Special Praise for *Relationship Sanity*

"*Relationship Sanity* is a roadmap to a thriving relationship. In their preceding book, *Irrelationship*, Borg and his colleagues located relationship insanity in couples' mutual fear of intimacy and all the ways they defend against closeness and vulnerability. In this book, to help couples face and transcend that fear, they make available a rich, detailed, and ultimately simple and doable process that helps couples to become present to each other, thus achieving and sustaining intimacy. Any couple will be enriched by using the myriad insights and exercises, and any therapist will be empowered to help couples by using them in their practice."

Harville Hendrix, PhD and Helen LaKelly Hunt, PhD, best-selling authors of *Getting the Love You Want* and *Making Marriage Simple*

"Borg, Brenner, and Berry have presented in this volume an accessible yet complex and sophisticated road map to assist couples, both those seemingly doing well and those in trouble, on the challenging journey to an intimate, rewarding, and sane relationship. Skillfully illuminating how early attachment strategies shape our adult assumptions about intimacy, the authors offer astutely designed exercises to be done by couples, alone and together, that will deepen understanding and awareness, for the self and for one another. Exposing and making sense of the hidden insecurities and conflicts most of us harbor about intimacy, the authors open up a compassionate path toward healing and growth. The wealth of knowledge and expertise here is immensely impressive and will certainly be of tremendous benefit to those couples ready to open themselves to the innate human potential for deeply satisfying intimacy."

Daniel Shaw, psychotherapist and author of Traumatic Narcissism: Relational Systems of Subjugation

"Filled with tips, exercises, and case studies, *Relationship Sanity* is a solidly researched approach to improving relationships through mindfully viewing your relationship as a third entity, separate from yourselves individually, which requires care and nurturing. It's a valuable tool whether you are beginning a relationship with a new partner or have been married and assumed you knew everything about your spouse."

Diana Kirschner, PhD, bestselling author of Love in 90 Days

RELATIONSHIP
SANITY

RELATIONSHIP
SANITY

Creating and Maintaining
Healthy Relationships

Mark B. Borg, Jr.

Grant H. Brenner

Daniel Berry

CENTRAL RECOVERY PRESS

LAS VEGAS

Central Recovery Press (CRP) is committed to publishing exceptional materials addressing addiction treatment, recovery, and behavioral healthcare topics.

For more information, visit www.centralrecoverypress.com.

© 2018 by Mark B. Borg, Jr., Grant Hilary Brenner, and John Daniel Berry
All rights reserved. Published 2018. Printed in the United States of America.

Publisher: Central Recovery Press
         3321 N. Buffalo Drive
         Las Vegas, NV 89129

23 22 21 20 19 18   1 2 3 4 5

Library of Congress Cataloging-in-Publication Data

Names: Borg, Mark B., Jr., author. | Brenner, Grant H., author. | Berry, Daniel, author.
Title: Relationship sanity : creating and maintaining healthy relationships / Mark B. Borg, Jr., Grant H. Brenner, Daniel Berry.
Description: Las Vegas : Central Recovery Press, [2018] | Description based on print version record and CIP data provided by publisher; resource not viewed.
Identifiers: LCCN 2018018096 (print) | LCCN 2018020441 (ebook) | ISBN 9781942094821 (ebook) | ISBN 9781942094814 (pbk. : alk. paper)
Subjects: LCSH: Intimacy (Psychology) | Interpersonal relations. | Interpersonal conflict.
Classification: LCC BF575.I5 (ebook) | LCC BF575.I5 B674 2018 (print) | DDC 158.2--dc23
LC record available at https://lccn.loc.gov/2018018096

Photos of Mark B. Borg, Jr., Grant Hilary Brenner, and John Daniel Berry by Eric Lee

Cover and interior design and layout by Deb Tremper, Six Penny Graphics

To Jonathan and Charlotte Rysanek, who have always lived in relationship sanity and have, therefore, shown me how to love and be loved.

Mark

For all who dare to love.

Grant

To Jack and Wilma, from whom I'm still learning about love.

Danny

Table of Contents

Introduction

What Is Relationship Sanity?

Many of us believe we want an honest, open-hearted relationship, but who really knows how to go about building one? In reality, this is a challenge for anyone who tries it.

Our first book, *Irrelationship: How We Use Dysfunctional Relationships to Hide from Intimacy*, explored that challenge in depth. In this follow-up, we will focus on proven, practical techniques for learning how to build the antithesis of irrelationship, called *relationship sanity*.

Many of us know the experience of feeling alone even while in romantic relationships. This may be related to feeling that we're doing all the giving while our partner is completely checked out—or vice versa! What had been mutual, intense excitement somehow gave way to something else. Where did our love go? Can we get it back?

Here you're going to read about couples who found themselves in that situation but learned to use the tools in this book to find their way back to a place of resurgent love—a place where love is able to thrive regardless of a history of disappointment, fear, and trauma.[1]

We have found in our work that there is a common but seldom articulated reality for many people: frightened as we may be of rejection and loneliness, many of us are even more frightened of what may happen if we're discovered and accepted for ourselves *as we really are.* The interdependence this implies often becomes intolerable, driving us into an irrelationship song-and-dance routine. How this maladaptive technique works will be explained in the pages that follow, but, as mentioned, it is covered in greater depth in *Irrelationship.*

This book, then, is for those of us seeking relationships of greater depth, honesty, and openness to what happens when we become vulnerable to one another in ways we may have considered impractical or even undesirable.

Here are examples of the couples featured in this book whose relationships changed dramatically as they discovered the way of relationship sanity.

- **Felicia and George** had lived "alone together" for years, having mastered the art of avoiding one another while living in the same house. This so obscured their commitment to one another that a severe crisis nearly resulted in divorce. But the tools of relationship sanity reconnected this middle-aged couple in ways long forgotten, leading them to reclaim their deep commitment to each other.

- **Ethan and Mia's** two-year marriage looked great to everybody around them, but they knew different. Somehow, each was aware of a growing distance that they didn't know how to bring up with one another. By using the tools in this book, however, they rediscovered their early passionate connection and found themselves more in love and more intimate than they'd thought possible.

- **Carol's wife Vanessa** was going through a period of deep pain and confused feelings about her own life. The worse Vanessa's pain became the more Carol distanced herself—to her own puzzlement. Was she being intentionally cruel and insensitive? By using the relationship sanity tools, Carol discovered that her emotional shutdown was connected to emotions left over from her early childhood. As she shared this discovery with Vanessa, the couple was able to share one another's history of unacknowledged pain, which brought new openness and joy to their marriage.

- **Ravi and Kamala** were in trouble, and they and everyone around them knew it. Then, one day during yet another argument about household finances, they unexpectedly started revealing to each other old, untapped feelings around money that dated from their childhood years. This led to a new, deeper connection that completely revitalized their marriage.

Also in the pages ahead, you will learn how to implement following the relationship sanity tools:
- Compassionate empathy
- Self-Other Help
- The 40-20-40 Model
- The DREAM Sequence

Building and maintaining relationships may be considered an art; and though we have scientific backgrounds, we invite you to approach this book creatively as artists, jointly constructing a relationship landscape that is a third entity[2]—an *us-ness* based on a reciprocal balance of giving and receiving—in which each person values and cares for the other. This requires curiosity and openness to wherever the process takes you in the journey of self-discovery, which is indispensable to figuring out why and how you drifted into the distancing techniques of irrelationship.

Jim and Emma

Jim and Emma are a couple whose marriage had almost every appearance of deep commitment to one another. But in reality, unconscious choices led to more and increasingly painful distance from one another.

"I didn't know where you'd gone," Emma reflected. "It made me angry, but sometimes I wondered if it were my fault. Until one day, I finally said it out loud: 'Jim, where have you gone?' And then, after a moment, I added, 'Where have *we* gone?'"

For his part, Jim believed he was doing everything he was supposed to do for his family, while at the same time feeling distressingly apart from them. When he and Emma talked about her two questions, he reflected, "If you hadn't finally put it into words, I don't know if I'd ever have been able to see how I'd put our whole life on hold. Of course, I was shocked by your statement, Emma, because you said this at the very moment I thought I was making more room for us—for our family."

So What Is Relationship Sanity?

Insanity has been defined as "doing the same thing over and over again and expecting different results," while sanity may be defined as "soundness of mind." In the irrelationship lexicon, *relationship sanity* may be defined as a balance of giving and receiving—reciprocity, mutuality, and alliance *in action*—and is created by experiencing oneself as loving and loveable. The insane part comes in when we invest ourselves in relationships that allow us to feel neither loved nor loveable, implicitly cut off from this feeling by a usually less-than-conscious blockage in the flow of giving and taking. While not appearing as floridly insane in most cases, irrelationship is the imbalance a couple creates together that deliberately excludes space for the open-hearted, reciprocal exchange of love characteristic of relationship sanity. Simply put, relationship sanity is a balance of giving and receiving in any relationship that has the potential for intimacy, empathy, vulnerability, and emotional investment.

We can part ourselves increasingly from relationship sanity by getting better and better at irrelationship, rather than critically examining what's actually happening in our relationship and seeking ways to curtail practices that don't work by replacing them with interaction techniques that do work—that promote mutual feelings of being loved and loveable.

"Something had started to change," Emma recalled. "Even the kids started to mention how Jim was around more, as if he was trying to make up for how far away he'd gotten. I was glad, of course, but something about it didn't seem quite right. He was being so in-your-face present and nice all the time that it made me nervous. But I was afraid of hurting his feelings, so I didn't say anything. Sometimes I half wished he'd go back to being away from home all the time; it was so weird. But the funny thing is we never really talked about it—not even to ask each other what we wanted from one another. Like we were afraid that would turn out to be a minefield. It finally turned into ignoring each other. It really wasn't nice. And, regardless of whatever it was we thought we wanted from each other, something was missing, something just wasn't right."

"Yeah," Jim responded, "I felt so guilty about being away all the time that I decided to make up for it by being the family hero. And I could tell that you didn't like it, though you never said anything. Looking back, we've both figured out that it was just another way I kept myself in the driver's seat. I dedicated myself to being present by working on and practicing being loving, kind, and generous to my family. I thought that was more than enough. I never considered how important it might be to allow others to offer these same things to me."

"And after you got that promotion," Emma said, "and were home every night, it wasn't long before I felt I may just as well not be there. You wouldn't let me do anything, interrupted every conversation I had with the kids, and wouldn't even hear me out when I tried to discuss what was happening, how things had changed. It was like nothing I felt or said even counted. I was feeling so lonely, Jim, so left out."

Irrelationship is a jointly created psychological defense system that two or more people maintain in order to avoid awareness of the anxiety that's a natural part of becoming close to others—especially anxiety about letting people see and know us for who we really are (i.e., intimacy). In irrelationship, one person is a Performer—in this case Jim, who is doing all the overt caretaking—and the other is the Audience—played by Emma in this relationship, who acts as if what the Performer as caretaker is giving is enough or is effective (even though it is not). Neither Performer nor Audience accept, take in, and make use of the *care* that the other is offering.

In fact, each defends her- or himself from doing just that via what we call *song-and-dance routines*—ways that compulsive caregiving is played out, or enacted, between people in a relationship.

"It was so odd to be doing so much for you, for our family, and still feel so left out—almost like you were working against me."

"And I might have been, Jim—I believed that wherever you'd been was far worse emotionally than where I'd been—I had the kids to keep me company, and I knew that I didn't want to feel what you felt."

"The ways that I experienced myself as being loving," Jim went on, "had everything to do with the things that I *do* for other people—the things I give. It never occurred to me that not allowing you to do the same for me would create an imbalance and ultimately have me questioning my own lovability."

"Right," admitted Emma, "I knew that your intentions were good. But there we were having survived some stretch of time when you were essentially gone, and you reappeared accepting nothing that I had to offer—not even the fact that I was still willing to accept you and work on fixing our relationship. I got it that you felt so unlovable, you made that very clear, but the ways that you were making up for it left no room for me, for us to really be—you know—us."

"I just couldn't see it, Emma. I think I was too scared."

"Actually, the closer you tried to be with me, the more it scared me."

Orbiting Our Partners

Is it possible to orbit around the heart of another in a so-called relationship—in a position of *either* giving *or* taking care—never taking in what others have to offer? Can we co-create a sustained orbit around each other where our positions never shift and never change?

In such a state, we cannot form a *healthy interdependence;*[3] we are safe in the insecurity of knowing—feeling and believing—that we can count on no one. This is a tightly knit control and a dynamic wherein we never get in (to the heart of another person), a place where no one gets in (to our heart).

The problem is not caregiving or care receiving because in irrelationship we only caretake—even if we do so by *acting as if* someone else's care is effective when it is not. Never accepting the offer, why would anyone resist loving and being loved? Perhaps because the invitation to accept care is also an invitation to empathize with our own history of love and loss.

We so often think about the high cost of *giving*—taxing us and exhausting our resources—but rarely do we consider the rip-off of disallowing others to give to us. When we do not accept, when we reject what others offer, we do not acknowledge or affirm the *value* of what it is that they have to give. The psychoanalyst and social psychologist Erich Fromm wrote, "Giving is the highest expression of potency. In the very act of giving, I experience my strength, my wealth, and my power. . . . Giving is more joyous than receiving, not because it is a deprivation, but because in the act of giving lies the expression of my aliveness."[4] The "protection" given us by irrelationship deprives ourselves and others of the pleasure of being both giver and receiver and the feeling of "aliveness" that's essential to sharing that experience.

"Funny," Jim said, "I never would have thought that being loveable was about anything other than believing that you love me—that you accept what I have to give. Now I can see that all the thinking in the world didn't equal accepting and taking in what you were trying to give to me, Emma."

Though in many cases, being loving and being lovable go together hand in glove, we see them as two separate and distinct directions that love can flow. In irrelationship, they don't flow, they collide—or endlessly chase each other's tails—and tend to create either a difficult-to-permeate boundary or a chronic chase scene. Either way, it is a defense, against what another seemingly "loving" person has to offer. In situations, like Emma and Jim's, where we are threatened by love's possibilities, as well as its anxieties and insecurities, it is easy to see how this hard-to-detect imbalance can simultaneously keep us safe *and* drive us crazy.

"I needed you to want and need me to be there—to be here—for you, Jim, or it just wasn't going to work."

"I didn't really understand," admitted Jim. "I had to ask Emma to explain, to help me. Asking for help became a kind of first step in allowing others to love me, to help me, to become important—maybe even essential—to me."

Because these are unconscious dynamics, we are generally unable to tell where the pain—the feeling of being ripped-off—is coming from. Insistent, persistent giving without allowing reciprocation becomes the goal, leaving no room for others to experience themselves as valuable contributors. The net result is that though everybody feels safe, everyone also loses, and, ultimately, feels vaguely and inexplicably angry—ironically, one is left feeling ripped off.

"I was more than willing to *help*," Emma said. "It was the first time that I felt Jim's presence even with all that mighty effort he was putting in to be a 'loving, generous, and kind' person."

"It turned out that being loving—without accepting my own wish or need to be loved—was not accepting conditions as they are. Only now, with a lot of help from Emma, am I coming to understand how I tried to control others, and my responses to them, by not accepting their care and love. Only now can I understand why so many people I've known have been so hurt and angry. Only now can I see how crazy I've been—how insane my relationships were."

Ironic as it may seem, loving in an "everything-flowing-outward" way is really no more validating to others than contempt. Repeatedly having one's desire to give triggers negative emotions, especially anger, as it did in Emma. Jim's hermetically-sealed giving routine protected him from seeing and feeling what others wanted to offer him. Fortunately, he became able to gradually understand that this left him in a terribly isolated emotional state.

The same was true for Emma. "I just missed him," she said, "and was beginning to believe he was never coming back."

Jim continued, "I put myself in solitary confinement. It was insane. And while the first step to sanity seemed simple, it turned out to be much harder to change than I thought it was going to be. But I began to listen.

Bit by bit I became open, willing, and finally able to accept and take in what Emma was offering me and let her love me."

"And," admitted Emma, "I realized that Jim didn't do this by himself: we'd allowed ourselves to drift further and further from what we now know is relationship sanity."

Exercise: Deep, Dark, Truthful Mirror *(Individuals)*

To attain a baseline for where you are—and where you were when you began this process—hit pause, reflect, and write down the very first thoughts, feelings, impressions, and reactions that you have to Emma and Jim's jailbreak from isolation to relationship sanity.

- Do you recognize yourself in this story?
- Do you relate to this story? If you do relate, can you do so through compassion and understanding? If you don't, what kind of assessment—perhaps even criticism—do you have for Jim, Emma, and their situation?
- What would you have done in Jim's situation? How about Emma's?
- What kind of recommendations do you have for Jim? For Emma? For their family?

Approaching Relationship Sanity from Irrelationship

Our previous book, *Irrelationship,* looks in depth at couples who, like Jim and Emma, jointly invested in irrelationship to avoid the anxiety related to the fear that their partners will learn too much about themselves—in other words, they're terrified by the prospect of intimacy.

In couples who use irrelationship, one party ordinarily acts as the Performer—in this case Jim, who was "caretaking" his wife and kids—while the other party, Emma, acts as the Audience by staying quiet about how uneasy Jim's distancing *and* caretaking made her. Together, they created a song-and-dance routine as a stand-in for the genuine opening of hearts that creates intimacy.

Irrelationship isn't apparent to outsiders, or even to the participants for that matter. Nothing seems wrong, but the imbalance between giving and taking stands directly in the way of building feelings of mutual love and safety with one another. In short, for such couples, relationship sanity is impossible.

But if the authenticity inherent in relationship sanity meets our genuine needs, why do so many of us resist it? The answer, put simply, is because relationship sanity exposes our vulnerability to one another and the anxiety that vulnerability creates. Allowing this exposure is to surrender control. Not surprisingly, many of us instead opt for the apparent safety—and denial—of irrelationship.

"It never occurred to me," Jim continued, "that trying to be nice to you and the kids would actually get in the way of feeling you loved me. But my performance as a hero was just driving a wedge between us."

Jim and Emma both learned the hard way that this kind of loving was only a short step from contempt, which was how Emma ultimately viewed Jim's heroics. Bad as his actions were, however, the feeling that she was losing—had lost—her life partner was even worse."

"I just missed you—missed you horribly."

"Yeah," Jim answered. "And all I'd really accomplished was putting myself in solitary confinement. It never for a minute hit me that shutting you out was how I locked myself in."

Self-sustaining, mutual isolation prevents our reaching one another's hearts as well as our own. This shields us from knowing about our partner's vulnerabilities, but it also blocks awareness of the pain as a result of our own histories of love and loss. This stalemate shuts down the possibility of giving and receiving. Thus it follows that irrelationship deprives our partners of the experience of aliveness that comes with true giving. Both partners pay a terrible price in choosing the safety of irrelationship.

And, Jim was surprised to learn how damaging this choice can be. "It never occurred to me that being loveable was about anything except what I have to give. And I sure never thought about how not letting you give would make you feel less loveable."

In irrelationship, loving and being loveable seem to be mutually exclusive, and attempts to frame it otherwise are confusing and frightening to those involved. The result is that both parties either repeatedly collide with each other or uselessly chase each other's tails. Either creates an impenetrable wall that prevents any gesture of genuine giving. This is the heartbreaking safety Jim and Emma lived in for years.

Emma summed up what she was feeling. "I needed you to want me to be there for you, Jim. Otherwise I couldn't see any reason to be married to you."

"Yeah. I was so wrapped up in my thing that I had no idea until you laid it out for me. Using you and the kids to prove what a great guy I was had nothing to do with being your partner."

Self-Other Help

Self-Other Help is a new paradigm for life change, distinct from the well-known self-help paradigm. Self-Other Help creates a safe space for truth telling and forgiveness that allows us to be who we really are with each other and opens the way for generosity and gratitude. It's no mistake that generosity and gratitude also represent the twin poles of a relationship: giving and receiving. The Self-Other Help Model is so profound that it dramatically reduces the likelihood of cover-ups, anxiety, guilt, and shame and creates a space in which the possibility of forgiving the unforgiveable becomes less remote.

When "you and I" have worked through irrelationship and reached relationship sanity, Self-Other Help takes account of that third entity—that third entity that is *us*. And, using the Self-Other Help Model as a means of achieving a living, breathing sense of us-ness in your everyday life is the primary task of this book.

Relationship Creativity and Play

Couples invested in irrelationship are stuck in rigid interactive roles that originated in relational patterns they developed with their earliest caregivers as a result of early childhood anxiety that threatened to become overwhelming. Even the idea of discussing anxiety-provoking issues is off-limits.

Probably the worst side effect of this rigid sidelining of feelings is that it shuts down the possibility of finding creative approaches to problem solving—especially when it comes to exploring interpersonal mishaps that could be defused with acceptance, mutual understanding, and even humor. The techniques of relationship sanity are a proven way out of this impasse.

Compassionate Empathy: The Key Ingredient of Self-Other Help

Compassionate empathy, the essential ingredient of relationship sanity, creates space for honest sharing that has the power to replace an anxiety-driven need for control. Compassionate empathy safely accesses the walled-off negative feelings that drove us into the irrelationship adaptation as small children.

Empathy can be compared to a powerful electrical source, while *compassion* acts as the regulator that keeps us from being electrocuted. Emma was afraid that if she allowed herself to feel empathy for Jim, she would herself become unsafe through loss of boundaries and perspective. Compassionate empathy ensures safety by promoting sharing of responsibility for what goes on in a relationship. When each partner maintains focus on his or her own feelings and experience without blaming or criticizing anyone else, compassionate empathy allows intimacy to develop in a way that defuses the fear of letting one's partner know too much about oneself.

Compassionate empathy is the doorway to intimacy and births mutuality, which allows someone else's experience—emotion—to inhabit our consciousness. Allowing that experience and emotion to *have life* in our consciousness and permitting ours to be taken in—accepted and cared for—by someone else is a two-person process. Compassionate empathy is the royal road that we, together, can trudge to cross the impossible distance between the head and the heart. It is a way to give *and* receive, to love *and* be loved, and, therefore, it is synonymous with—the very definition of—relationship sanity. Its vehicle is active listening—a practice that, in our connected world has become, at best, unnecessary and, at worst, obsolete. Another benefit of compassionate empathy is that it unlocks *brainlock,* i.e. the psychological, neurobiological, interpersonal, and social-contextual factors that keep us stuck in the habit of irrelationship.[5]

Relationship sanity is necessarily relational: since we created irrelationship with another person or persons, the antidote is sharing experience and exploring history using compassionate empathy. Healthiness thus includes a shared state of being in a reciprocal relationship with the world as represented by other people.[6]

Self-Awareness and Self-Other Help

Developing a sense of ourselves in context of relationships passes through several stages, as defined by Carnes, Laaser, and Laaser:[7]
   1. **Dependence:** We need and want help.
   2. **Counterdependence:** We need help but resist it.
   3. **Independence:** We are self-sufficient and do not need help.
   4. **Interdependence:** We both give and receive help.

Interdependence is obviously a vital aspect of relationship sanity, while compulsive caretaking can look a lot like the first three phases of dependence. *Dissociation* is the term psychoanalysts use for defense mechanisms that block, deny, and cut ourselves off from awareness of our need for help. The path of relationship sanity is a process of *association* or *reassociation.* Along this path, we learn to tolerate, accept, and finally embrace Self-Other Help as normal, healthy, human experience. Compassionate empathy is the mechanism that opens this door to relationship sanity.

Compassionate empathy ratchets down our need to use blame, cover-up, and shame when negotiating relationship issues, thus clearing space for gratitude, open-heartedness, and forgiveness—more constructive approaches. This doesn't happen all at once, of course, but by using this book, couples can learn skills that completely change how they process issues, although those new skills probably won't feel all that good at first, even when the couple shares a conscious desire to stop harming one another.

Song-and-Dance Routines

As mentioned previously, the mechanics of irrelationship are called the song-and-dance routine. These routines are basically *enactments*, a psychoanalytical term for acting out unconscious feelings in the form of behaviors that play out what is happening without the benefit of putting dynamics into words so that such patterns can be meaningful and transformative for those involved.[8] Song-and-dance routines allow us to keep our distance from the anxiety we feel as we approach of the possibility of intimacy.

The Make-Up of Irrelationship

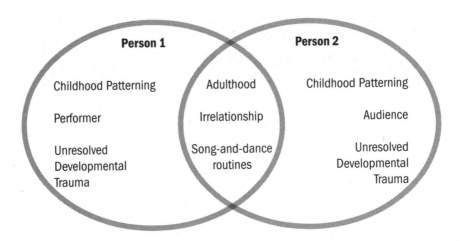

Person 1

Childhood Patterning

Performer

Unresolved Developmental Trauma

Adulthood

Irrelationship

Song-and-dance routines

Person 2

Childhood Patterning

Audience

Unresolved Developmental Trauma

As illustrated in the diagram, a couple jointly creates and perpetuates irrelationship. Similarly, health and well-being are created in relation to others. Patterns of self-care and how we care for others are reflections of how our primary caregivers (usually our parents) took care of us as small children.

Irrelationship theory is grounded in Harold Searles' hypothesis that human beings are natural-born caretakers.[9] And John Bowlby, the progenitor of attachment theory, found that human beings have an inborn motivation to be *care-seekers*.[10] Thus, we have an inborn desire to heal the wounds of those around us—especially those of our primary caregivers on whom we depend for security and comfort. Ironically, when a parent is disturbed, a turning of the tables—a reverse caretaking—can occur that creates what can be considered a *developmental trauma* that creates a defensive caretaking operation that blocks genuine reciprocal giving and receiving. Once the defensive pattern is assumed, the individual carries it forward through life, playing it out in many types of relationships that, in some manner, represent security.[11]

Irrelationship exploits the ambivalence many of us feel when faced with the possibility of intimacy, especially toward someone to whom we're genuinely attracted. Often the connection is allowed to progress to increasing attachment and commitment, despite our ambivalence. Even in these cases, however, unresolved intimacy-based anxiety doesn't just dissipate: affected couples unconsciously create a song-and-dance routine that ensures that neither party is at risk for exposing their vulnerability to each other.

If, in addressing irrelationship, one of the members of a couple focuses only on her or his feelings and needs, she or he risks reinforcing defenses that stand in the way of intimacy. An added risk of not doing the work together is that if one person is making progress in individual therapy but the other person is not on the same track, the relationship will probably suffer when only one person's communication skills improve. On the other hand, couples who work at change together are more likely to be successful.

Hiding from Relationships

The following is an exchange with an anonymous reader of our *Psychology Today* blog. The reader was responding to the blog entry entitled, "Hiding from Relationship—in Relationship." The exchange illustrates how our collaborative model, the 40-20-40, works.

Reader: Thanks for your blog, but I have some questions.

If irrelationship is an emotional defense system created by two people (and I believe that to be true), so too wouldn't it necessitate the active participation of the two "creators" to resolve this block to intimacy? You've cogently described the reasons for, and behaviors of, participating in irrelationship. And you've also alluded to the fear (maybe even terror for some people) that is involved in the possibility of being and revealing one's true self. I get all that.

I'm not sure I fully understand the steps toward achieving what one wants (as in "wanting out"), not necessarily wanting out of the partnership/marriage but wanting out of the song-and-dance. It's fortunate when both parties desire change. But, in some cases, it may be unrealistic to assume both partners want change at the same time. And therein lies the rub. I appreciated your comment about needing courage to forge ahead with one's intention of reframing a painfully unhealthy partnership. How challenging it is, though, to be alone in the irrelationship, and, also, to be alone in the desire to change the relationship into something more real and intimate!

It's not just "breaking up is hard to do." When a person chooses to confront an emotional defense structure so deeply embedded in two lives, it becomes an excruciating confrontation with a life orientation built to protect oneself from that original pain that set the whole thing in motion. And if you really think about it, this terror is not about a marriage break-up; it's about allowing oneself to feel that early experience that created an emotional lifestyle. It's about tolerating what one most fears—the "I don't want you as you really are" blow to the heart.

Authors: Thank you for your thoughtful and thought-provoking response to our recent blog entry. We've been—and are—finding that recovery from the irrelationship routine, just like starting it up and keeping it up, as you suggest, is a process that requires the proverbial "two to tango." And so we see that the development of irrelationship theory and working through its straitjacket-for-two suggest a new category: instead of a traditional self-help perspective, irrelationship requires work better described as Self-Other-Help.

One of the tools we're developing for couples is called the 40-20-40 Model.[12] It was inspired by and adapted from a practice called Group Process Empowerment. It creates a space for addressing each partner's anxiety-driven contribution to the routine. For example, each party articulates what she or he contributes both to the problem and to the solution, and both parties take the opportunity to examine how their individual histories interlock to create a defense system. This process of self-inventory and naming aloud what each partner finds begins the process of creating a new shared safety within which members can build genuine, reciprocal collaboration and ownership of relationship sanity.

Unfortunately, as you suggested, many people invested in irrelationship trip on taking the first "shot" at what seems like a Russian-roulette gamble to find out if, underneath their defense routines, they'll find a partner who will accept them as they really are. But this is only the first dilemma. Another haunting fear of people who have depended on irrelationship is that we'll find out how invested we are in shared life with our partner, all the while realizing that, no matter how invested we may feel, we have no guarantee of success. In fact, our history is probably a salient indicator of how easy it would be for us to blow it.

People who have relied on irrelationship for safety can become able to listen to the signals—sometimes longstanding signals—that something isn't right and agree to take on the work of recovery. Some people will, of course, flee at the prospect of disclosing their fears to one another. Others will opt to return to the denial and isolation of their song-and-dance routines, silently resigned to the gnawing apprehension that's part of their everyday lives.

The primary task in irrelationship work, which your response to the blog brings us back to, is to expand awareness of the myriad ways irrelationship affects us and to point the way toward recovery. The Self-Other tools maintain our focus on the deficits inherent in irrelationship while keeping the door open for building genuine relationships. If we stay with the process we have a good chance of finding our way to true intimacy—and into relationship sanity.

Using This Book

This book is organized into two parts.

- **Part One: Relationship Sanity versus Irrelationship** reviews the anatomy of irrelationship, so you can understand how we sabotage the possibility of love and intimacy and how we can replace bad, old habits by using the Self-Other Assessment.

- **Part Two: The Way of Relationship Sanity: The DREAM Sequence** teaches you how to use the DREAM Sequence, a five-step model for recovery from irrelationship. The sequence leads couples through the process of opening their hearts in order to recapture what attracted them to each other to begin with, ultimately deepening their commitment to each other.

Anyone who is single or partnered, and has read this far or read our previous book or our blog, and is struck even slightly by what they've read is likely to benefit from the content of the following chapters. However, this book is framed as a guide for couples who have become aware of an unaccountable distancing in their shared lives that they want to undo.

The exercises in this book probe for a detailed relationship history. This part of the process might best be undertaken apart from one's partner. Having your own copy of the book allows you to annotate, mark, and write freely as questions and issues arise. A journal may be useful for detailed recollections and reflection.

When a section or exercise has been completed, the couple shares their results as candidly as possible with each other. Becoming comfortable doing this may not be easy at first. When sharing, keep eye and ear open for complementary findings as well as conflicts that need further examination.

As you move forward as a couple, you can expect to relearn things about one another that you had forgotten and discover new significance to traits that you hadn't considered previously. The goal is to forge a stronger bond and rediscover your excitement about being together using compassionate empathy. The learning tasks and benefits of compassionate empathy include

- understanding the true nature of the "us" in your relationship by bringing to light patterns of relating that either strengthen or undermine connection;
- learning to view your relationship *as a third entity*, separate from yourselves individually, that requires care and nurture;
- becoming able to live in and with the ambiguity of intimacy and vulnerability;

- viewing relationship sanity not as a goal but as a technique for nurturing your connection.

A Few More Suggestions

As you embark on your rediscovery, put aside regular times to work both individually and together as couple and *stick with them.*

When you feel uneasy or are resisting doing the work, let your partner know. Candor will help reduce resistance and improve your shared commitment to doing the work.

Do not rush. The exercises in each chapter build trust for the process itself, so set aside time when you don't have to watch the clock.

Welcome to the beginning of *Relationship Sanity!*

Part One

Relationship Sanity versus Irrelationship

Chapter 1

Not Wanting What We Think We Want

"I should have known that something was badly wrong when Mason pulled out Henry Miller's trilogy *The Rosy Crucifixion* (totaling 1,462 pages) on our honeymoon."

At some unconscious level, the couple living in irrelationship finds "safety" in knowing what they can expect from one another and what *not* to ask for. It's kind of like an old joke cultural theorist Slavoj Žižek likes to tell about Communist Poland.[1]

> A customer enters a store.
>
> Customer: "Do you have any butter?"
>
> Clerk: "No, we're the store that doesn't have any toilet paper. The store across the street is the one that doesn't have any butter!"

Gina and Mason knew they didn't have to worry that either would ask the other for closeness and sharing—an idea that scared the daylights out of them. This made it easy for Gina to blame their disappointing honeymoon on Mason's busy-ness with Henry Miller, with the added value of giving her an out for dealing with her anxiety about whether or not she was sexually desirable. This configuring of their marriage may seem insane, but remaining blind to their song-and-dance routine enabled Gina and Mason to keep themselves blissfully unaware of their fear of intimacy.

"I'd spent years pretending I was okay with a sexless relationship, which let me off the hook from confronting Mason about it. But deciding to get married changed something for me, and I decided I was going to *ask for it* on our honeymoon. Well, Mason didn't even try to pretend he wanted me more than he wanted Henry Miller. After six years together, I was finally forced to swallow the hard truth that he didn't *want* to be close to me that way. If I wanted sex, I'd have to go elsewhere. And, well, that's what I ended up doing.

"Still, it was a real shame: all those trips to Victoria's Secret, having some naughty fun buying naughty nightie things—things I ended up wearing to monitor Mason's progress through *Rosy Crucifixion.* If I'm honest, though, I knew a long time ago that Mason just wasn't a very romantic guy—not the way everybody dreams of, I guess. So where did I get the idea that he loved me—or that I wanted him to love me?"

This wasn't the first time this had happened to Gina. "I finally admitted to myself that our honeymoon was actually a replay of what happened with every boyfriend I'd had since high school. Then I heard about irrelationship—about people who were really afraid of letting anyone get too close, no matter how attracted to the other person they were, so I finally started wondering, 'Am I doing this on purpose?'".

For Gina, the upside of hitting the wall on their honeymoon was that it forced her to admit that the "same ol' same ol'" wasn't working anymore, which is—or can be—the jumping off place for relationship sanity. So, while Mason wasn't especially interested in changing their status quo, Gina's investment in their song-and-dance routine drained away pretty quickly.

In many cases, however, a couple becomes able to break through that denial together and admits that something is wrong—and they want to fix it. In such cases, the couple

1. recognizes their mutual isolation;
2. decides together that they want to recover what excited them about each other when they first met;

3. breaks free from the straitjacket of their song-and-dance routines;
4. faces and works through the buried feelings and fears that had overwhelmed their ability to be there for one another.

Often, opening the door to buried anxiety can be harrowing, and deciding to do so doesn't guarantee a restored relationship. But the agreement to go through it together, *no matter what,* gives the couple a better shot at the outcome they're hoping for.

Exercise: Joint Compassion Meditation[2]—Learning to Observe Thoughts and Feelings

In this brief section, we outline some basic moves for establishing a practice which you—as partners in a building alliance—can create and then return to at certain suggested key points and/or any time the work in this book becomes anxiety-provoking and overwhelming. We suggest putting a sticky-note on this page because we'll ask users to return to this exercise a few times in the course of the book.

Observing our thoughts and feelings nonjudgmentally as spectators isn't something many of us practice, despite evidence of the value of doing so. But cultivating this practice—sometimes known as *mindfulness*—and using it in stressful situations helps us focus on essential information needed to make better choices, including choices about how to navigate relationships. At times, you and your partner may find it necessary to do this exercise in separate rooms or even at separate times.

- Start in a comfortable, seated position with your feet flat on the floor, your head slightly tilted down, and your eyes partially open, focusing on a spot a few feet in front of you. Avoid falling asleep.
- Sit quietly giving attention to the breath while observing without judgment the stream of thoughts passing through your mind. Then return your attention to the breath.

- Since this is not a competition or contest, even against yourself, there is no good/bad or right/wrong: it's simply a process for learning about what your mind does and becoming able to step back from it.
- Now, together and using a timer, spend three to five minutes sitting quietly and looking into one another's eyes. You may find the following questions useful.
    - o How did it feel to observe your thoughts and emotions without reacting to them?
    - o What suggestions or reflections can you offer one another about observing thoughts without reacting to them?
- When you share your experience, speaking and listening without interruption, use *compassionate listening*.
- As you listen, with each inhalation, imagine compassion is flowing into you, from the world, and from you to yourself.[3] As you exhale, imagine that compassion is flowing from you into your partner. You may do this whenever listening and especially throughout the exercises in the following chapters.
- After your session, no matter how brief, make notes about how it felt, what you thought about, and how this practice might relate to learning how to be present in your relationship.

Identifying Emotions

"It's seems strange now," Mason reflected, "that both of us were too afraid to ask each other for what we wanted. Anyway, I know I was: I learned not to ask for anything when I was growing up. Our family life was such a mess that somehow I knew the safest thing to do was to just keep my head down. Well, what a mess *that* made for me *and* Gina. I knew Gina was getting hurt but I was paralyzed. I just couldn't reach out to her. I excused it by reminding myself that when we first met, she told me how afraid she was of getting too close. Boy, did that come in handy. I used that to let myself off the hook for years."

"Yeah," Gina added. "And I was just wishing that he'd show feelings about something, anything, to break up how boring our lives had become."

"Well somehow, I finally got it," Mason said, "and when I did, I felt so bad that I was willing to do pretty much anything to figure out how we'd gotten into this dead space of just existing with one another. Thank God, I could still tell that I really loved Gina and wanted to be with her. I wanted to stop that damned dance around our marriage. I just didn't know what to do different."

The breaking through of uncomfortable feelings is probably the most recognizable first sign that irrelationship isn't working anymore. The good news is that the more uncomfortable those feelings are the more likely the couple still has something worth keeping.

The lengths to which we'll go to prevent others from knowing too much about us is particularly problematic in romantic relationships. But the desire to shield ourselves from exposing our vulnerability and dependence to others can also be isolating among family members, disruptive among coworkers, and counterproductive in any setting where individuals undertake a shared task.

The following exercises focus on how we came to defend ourselves from those on whom we depend. We do this by looking at what it *feels like* to depend on others, why this makes us feel anxious, and finally by beginning to examine the behaviors we developed to deal with these uncomfortable feelings.

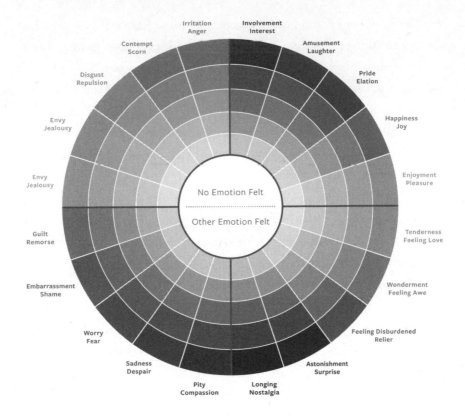

Exercise: Naming Feelings *(Individuals and Couples)*

During this exercise, you will learn to identify and get to the bottom of strange or unwanted feelings. This is a vital skill for overcoming feelings of isolation. Refer to the Emotion Wheel on this page to help guide your discussion.

- Recall a serious argument you had with your partner and write down as accurately as you can what each party said as the disagreement proceeded.
- What emotions came up most often and what was happening when they did? Distinguish between feelings you showed and didn't show.
- Make note of feelings both of you had during the disagreement, simultaneously or not. How did this commonality of feelings affect the argument?

Now review the argument you detailed.

- Identify exchanges that sound like avoidance (irrelationship) as opposed to honest sharing (relationship sanity).
- Do any themes stand out in the argument? Which ones?
- Identify implicit or explicit messages you were giving each other.
- Having examined this exchange, what would you like to change? How would you do that?

Associating and Reassociating

Feelings of pain and loneliness, missing each other, and anger at feeling abandoned are warning signs that irrelationship defenses are no longer defending us from our dissociated feelings. Reassociating blocked experience requires compassion for ourselves and our partner if healing is to take place.

Compassionate empathy entails honestly sharing our deepest anxieties and vulnerability with someone who is important in our life—feelings that we've deliberately kept out of our own sightlines since we were small children. Such sharing requires mutual generosity and gratitude—the antithesis of the one-sidedness of an irrelationship song-and-dance routine.

Approaching Our Fears

Anxiety can make us overanalyze problems, making our anxiety worse and hampering our ability to verbalize our feelings and solve problems. The result is that we'll probably return to our default setting of suppressing our feelings, which aggravates the harm done by ongoing anxiety.

The information and exercises that follow are aimed at moving you from anxiety to acceptance of feelings and, ultimately, toward compassionate empathy, the foundation of relationship sanity.

Cognitive Distancing: Our ability to make quick decisions is a skill we developed tens of thousands of years ago to survive life-or-death situations. However, as mentioned previously, split-second decision-making can be cluttered by an unending stream of emotional reactions to information buzzing around in our minds. Pausing and stepping back from that buzzing improves our attempt at better decision-making in stressful situations.

Focusing on Direct Experience: Our minds create stories about how safe and loveable we are based on experiences we had with our first caregivers. As we begin to detach from what goes through our minds, we become able to identify and question assumptions about ourselves and the world. This improves our readiness and ability to encounter life-experiences and other people with acceptance and spontaneity. The following practice allows you to explore the present spontaneously and without overthinking.

- What is "right now" like?
- Where is your mind's focus right now? Is it on what's *actually* happening, what *might* happen, or on what *has* happened?
- What's the difference between what's actually happening and what you think or fear might happen?
- What's the difference between how you feel when you think about what's actually happening and when you think about what might happen?
- What role does fear play in your relationship with your partner? What about in other aspects of your life?

Exercise: Labeling *(Individuals and Couples)*

This exercise examines how your thoughts get in the way of actual experience.

1. Reflect on the thoughts you noted in the "Naming Feelings" exercise and write down a few words to describe the content of those thoughts.

2. Discuss (or write about) how your thoughts may reveal what's going on in your head and how they might interfere with being present with a person or experience "right now." Take note of how labels you give your thoughts might shape or reflect your true feelings and how you honestly view a situation.

Exercise: Staying in the Present *(Couples)*

One of the main indicators of irrelationship is the repetition of patterns used in unsuccessful relationships. While our past failures are not guarantees that we'll repeat them, failure to intervene consciously will likely result in our continuing to edge away from our true desires.

The following exercise can lessen the power the past has over you.

1. Set a timer. Take three to five minutes apart from one another to reflect on your past, both before and since you met your partner.
2. Come together again and reflect on how the exercises you've done up to this point are affecting your understanding and experience of being with another person.
3. Discuss the idea of being in a relationship as a choice rather than a solution to a problem, such as your fear of being alone or the feeling that you need someone to take care of you.
4. Discuss any new ideas or feelings you have about the idea of losing a relationship.

Exercise: Broadening the View *(Couples)*

Compassionate empathy is a technique for building intimacy by listening in hospitable silence—the foundation of relationship sanity.

1. Discuss new insights you're gaining about how anxiety related to past experiences affects how you see others and react to interpersonal situations.
2. Identify simple tools from the exercises that might be useful for countering anxiety-provoking situations *while you're in them.*

Exercise: Remembering the First Encounter *(Couples)*

How did your relationship start? What was it about this person that got under your skin and stayed there? Did it happen fast, or did it take time? Did you have reservations or did it seem perfect?

The following questions will help you reflect on the beginning of your relationship. Take time to sit and ask and answer the questions together.

1. What was it like when we met?
2. Where did we meet?
3. How old were you and what was going on in your life?
4. How long was your previous relationship, and how long had you been single (if you were) when you met?
5. How did your meeting come about?
6. Was there anything about meeting each other that felt familiar? If yes, how did you feel about that?
7. When you met, did you think you saw qualities in your partner that have turned out to be accurate? Which qualities turned out to be inaccurate?

Write down anything else about your first meeting(s) that stand out in your mind—especially feelings or behaviors. Avoid censoring yourself. Compare your results noting points of agreement and disagreement. Take note of questions raised as well as items you prefer to avoid discussing.

Exercise: There Was Something About You (Couples)

Now let's drill down into what happened on your first meeting. Answer these questions individually.

1. What traits do you remember as first catching your attention?
   a. Physical traits or overall appearance
   b. Particular emotional or other non-verbal signals
   c. The way she or he conversed or shared ideas
   d. Purely or almost purely sexual
   e. Unable to be put into words? If so, try to do so now.
2. What initial attractions remain appealing to you?
3. What initial attractions or traits have either disappeared or turned out to be erroneous?

Next write a detailed description of what made your partner exciting to you. Was it something emotional, intellectual, physical, or spiritual? Did you like his or her sense of humor? Did she or he make you feel safe? If you felt only sexual attraction at first, discuss that and describe how that changed or didn't change.

Now share your responses with each other. Discuss similarities and differences.

1. How does it feel *right now* to be doing this with each other?
2. Are you aware of leaving out anything important? Do you know why you did?
3. Are you aware *right now* of feelings you had about or for each other when you first met? What is it like to recall them?

Staying on Target: Connected versus Estranged

By now, you're probably coming to realize that examining the same problems over and over again isn't necessarily the way you're going to solve them. In fact, doing so may just feed your anxiety, making it even harder to find solutions.

When your mind is stuck in a loop, you can interrupt it by getting up and moving around or doing a different task or activity. When you sit down again, you should have a different perspective. Truth be told, that's what you have been doing together as you work on the exercises in this chapter. What's it been like? *Getting up and getting going*—not staying stuck in your thoughts and your song-and-dance routines—has been driven by the compassionate empathy and opening up to intimacy that you unlocked and brought forth at the moment you agreed to work with each other—to *help* in a *reciprocal* way.

Key Takeaways

- We can be kind to ourselves and to each other in this moment.
- We can give each other the compassionate empathy needed to feel accepted and cared for by each other.
- Compassionate empathy can allow us to reach, touch, and be touched by each other.

- We can break out of isolation together.
- We can verbalize thoughts or phrases expressive of our immediate situation—perhaps returning to the feelings we were experiencing when we began—hurt, sadness, or anger. Then we can verbalize the desire to use that negative experience as an opening to a compassionately empathetic relationship.

Through these means, we can break out of our fear and isolation. We will learn that a healthy relationship is developed and maintained to withstand our conflicts, our ambivalence, and our insecurity—that is, relationship sanity is the place where we are ultimately loved, cared for, and accepted as we actually are.

Now pause and look at each other. Use free association to discuss any thoughts or thought fragments, feelings, reflections, and analysis of where you were and where you're headed—individually and as a couple—along the road of recovery from irrelationship, the road of relationship sanity.

Chapter 2

Drilldown: How Irrelationship Works

An irrelationship routine is the outgrowth of patterns a person develops as a small child to relieve her or his primary caregivers' anxiety so that the caregiver is able to meet the child's emotional needs. The caregiver then comes to depend on the child to provide this kind of "caretaking." If this dynamic doesn't change, the child will unconsciously continue this caretaking pattern into adulthood, approaching romantic partners and others as someone for whom she or he *must* perform a caretaking role and on whom she or he depends to act the part of an appreciative audience. Underlying this pattern is a shared wariness of close relationships that short-circuits genuinely intimate relationships.

Hiding from Relationship—in Relationship

Will and Kimberly came from families in which showing feelings or complaining about unmet needs was off-limits. As a result, neither was prepared for intimacy with a romantic partner, which made the unhappy outcome of their marriage all but inevitable.

The thrill of their early courtship never developed into actual intimacy either before or after they were married. After four years together, both felt isolated and subtly devalued; however having never learned skills for sharing feelings and fears, they weren't able even to bring up the mutual feeling that their connection was fading.

What short-circuited Kimberly and Will's connection? Received wisdom says that early excitement naturally and inevitably fades as familiarity grows. However, as psychoanalyst Stephen Mitchell cautions us, this may be related to choosing to cultivate stability in a relationship we depend on instead of repeatedly opting for partnerships characterized by "episodic, passionate idealization," which he views as "a dangerous business."[1]

When anxiety controls our relational styles, we're uneasy around spontaneity, self-disclosure, and the unpredictability of passion. Children who grow up in households that discourage spontaneity and reciprocity are likely to grow into adults who demand carefully scripted romantic relationships. Families in which discussion of emotions or needs isn't allowed are likely to produce adults who haven't the skills to process even their own feelings. Typically such individuals lack capacity for genuine caregiving or constructively addressing rough spots in relationships.

Connections based on these deficits often appear to be lopsided: one person's needs appear to determine the other's behavior. One party performs and the other accepts and even applauds what the other gives. But in reality, the parties are equally invested in warding off unpredictable feelings and events.

Kimberly and Will's song-and-dance routine was configured along these lines:

- You'll accept whatever I do for you and act as if you're grateful for it.
- I'll act as if you're fun to be with and "that's what's so special about you."
- Our interactions will carefully skirt around real issues without us ever indicating that we're aware we're doing so.

In a matter of months, Kimberly and Will each felt abandoned by the other, yet neither could have explained why or how. But instead of reaching out to one another, they clung to two rules they'd learned as children: (1)

Ignore my unmet needs and negative feelings, and (2) Don't ask questions about your needs and desires. Ultimately, this was a price too high that left them burned out and wanting out. Their marriage ended, Will observed, with a thud rather than an explosion.

Exercise: Caretaking Agreements (*Couples*)

This table provides examples of caretaking agreements in a relationship and is followed by questions to help you clarify characteristics of your own relationship that are markers of irrelationship.

Caretaking Agreement Examples	How Do We Feel in the Relationship	What Is Its Impact on Our Relationship
I diligently provide caretaking for my partner who needs a lot of help.	I feel resentful and overburdened; you feel resentful and unappreciated.	Our roles deflect conflict and in them we feel increasingly estranged, but we can't see any way to address issues or solve problems.
I accept my partner's caretaking whether it meets my needs or not.	I feel unheard and unable to express what I need. You try even harder and don't seem to listen to what I say. Nothing really seems to make me feel better.	We've lost touch with the feelings that brought us together; we feel uneasy without knowing why; and we see no other options and feel hopeless.

What kinds of agreements, conscious or not, have you made with each other about what behaviors are acceptable for you to offer one another? Using the previous table as a guide, discuss unspoken agreements you see yourself and your partner living by and how these agreements play out in your day-to-day lives.

Creating a safe space for discussing relationship roles and other anxiety-provoking subjects is the primary tool for building relationship sanity. The following statements will help bring significant markers of irrelationship into focus. After answering each numbered item individually, share and compare your responses.

1. I should be the solution to my partner's life. (My partner should really "need" me.)
   a. Agree
   b. Not sure or sometimes
   c. Disagree

2. My partner should be the answer to what I need in my life. (My partner will solve all my problems.)
   a. Agree
   b. Not sure or sometimes
   c. Disagree

3. Love mostly means taking care of my partner. (I want someone who needs me to look after him.)
   a. Agree
   b. Not sure or sometimes
   c. Disagree

4. Love means my partner is always there to take care of me. (My partner is always around to make sure I'm okay.)
   a. Agree
   b. Not sure or sometimes
   c. Disagree

5. When I'm taking care of my partner, I sometimes feel unappreciated. (My partner doesn't realize all I do for him or doesn't value it enough.)
   a. Agree
   b. Not sure or sometimes
   c. Disagree

6. Things are too one-sided between my partner and me. (I do all the giving, and she just takes.)
    a. Agree
    b. Not sure or sometimes
    c. Disagree

7. Being in a relationship is more work than pleasure. (Having a partner drains me and leaves me feeling unfulfilled.)
    a. Agree
    b. Not sure or sometimes
    c. Disagree

8. My partners have usually been women or men who didn't really listen to me. (My partner doesn't take a lot of trouble to make herself available and to reassure me.)
    a. Agree
    b. Not sure or sometimes
    c. Disagree

9. Overall, my relationships with partners have been disillusioning.
    a. Agree
    b. Not sure or sometimes
    c. Disagree

The more you agree with these statements the more likely it is that you look for partners who view caretaking as a baseline expectation for a relationship, which is highly suggestive that irrelationship figures prominently in how you seek to construct relationships with romantic partners and others—including family members.

In the exercises and chapters that follow, we'll look at what traits you consider desirable in partners and friends versus traits that make you feel uneasy or frighten you.

Key Players

The roles defining irrelationship are the *Performer* and the *Audience*.

- The **Performer** is the overt caretaker who appears to be calling the shots by deciding how the Audience needs to be helped and creating a caretaking routine to fill that need.
- The **Audience**, the apparently passive receiver of the Performer's help, is actually caretaking the Performer by appearing to accept and benefit from whatever she or he offers.

The Price of Quieting Our Anxiety

When anxiety is well managed, we feel, think, and function better. But when we handle anxiety—or any other feeling simply by blocking our awareness of it—we risk losing guidance of *all* our emotions because our minds don't allow us to pick and choose which feelings to ignore. If you numb one, you risk numbing them all.

But the feelings don't just go away: sooner or later, some experience apparently unrelated to our denied feelings will trigger an overwhelming emotional reaction that will seem to come out of nowhere. Such experiences ultimately do little to relieve unaddressed anxiety.

Dysfunctional Behaviors Used to Quiet Anxiety

As mentioned previously, adults continue song-and-dance routines learned in childhood to manage feelings of anxiety associated with would-be intimate relationships. But this mechanism only suppresses *awareness*—not the feelings themselves—so that the disturbing impact of those feelings continues in the unconscious mind without our knowing it.

In many cases, suppressing the awareness of anxiety is jointly and tacitly agreed upon by the whole family. Sometimes one family member takes on a monitoring role and has the job of creating a distraction when she or he senses that anxiety is approaching an "unsafe" level, thus allowing the family's emotional equilibrium to return to "normal." Often, the person taking on that role continues it throughout her or his life.

Exercise: Dysfunctional Behavior *(Individuals)*

The following table looks at behaviors commonly used to block awareness of anxiety, who performs the behaviors, and their impact. For each example, read from left to right to appreciate the underlying dynamics and purpose of the dysfunctional behavior.

Dysfunctional Behavior	Who Used the Behavior and Why	Target or Recipient of the Behavior	Impact of the Behavior
Speaking disparagingly about neighbors; comparing them to our family	Mother usually instigated with the whole family joining in to distract us from uncomfortable feelings we had toward each other.	Whole family	Created one-sided negative feelings that isolated us from neighbors
Ignoring parents' drug use	Daughters maintained image that home life was stable and safe. Daughters avoid discussing parents' drug use or its effects on family life with each other; pretended everything was fine.	Each other, friends, neighbors, teachers	Unmet needs resulted in inability to concentrate, inadequate hygiene, poor diet, poor grades, and social isolation

Using the previous table as a guide, analyze your most significant relationships.

- What dysfunctional behaviors of your own can you identify from the past and present that affect how you relate to others?
- How might those behaviors have developed as a result of experiences you had growing up?
- What behaviors in people close to you can you identify that kept them at a "safe" distance from others?

- How does that history connect with your own self-protective song-and-dance routine?

Attachment Style and Self-Other Experience

High-functioning people appear emotionally sturdy and secure, while those affected by irrelationship have locked down their feelings to conceal what psychoanalysts call an *insecure attachment style*. This lockdown limits access to self-other experience—that is, limits perception of ourselves and others in (potentially) intimate relationships.

Research has identified a relationship between individuals' experiences with caregivers as children and how they connect with others as adults.[2] The façade created by people affected by irrelationship deflects their attention from anxiety related to poor caregiving they received as small children. Identifying this anxiety is essential to dealing with the fear driving irrelationship.

Insecure attachment styles may also be described as either avoidant or anxious, respectively, depending on the quality of empathy that had existed between child and caregiver, the child's innate traits, and the fit between the child and the attachment styles of the child and caregiver.[3]

People with a secure attachment style remain essentially grounded during emotional disruptions and even during severe life crises. They typically weather such experiences without becoming derailed, even in cases of deep disturbance, returning relatively quickly to equilibrium and growing as a result of the experience.

By contrast, people with insecure attachment styles experience the normal ups and downs of life as so anxiety provoking that they either ignore or avoid them or become preoccupied with them. In both cases, they're often unable to work through and integrate feelings and conflicts productively, so they defend themselves by avoiding real interpersonal connections or confrontations. At the same time, they may unreflectively jump into relationships that seem magically to offer relief or solve problems without much effort.

The interplay between two people with insecure attachment style is prone to snowballing rapidly into a crisis. For example, if an adult who avoids intimacy gets involved with someone who is preoccupied with a potential partner, the avoidant person will increasingly retreat from the other, provoking an increasingly anxiety-driven pursuit by the preoccupied person. This creates a cycle whose resolution is usually unpleasantly dramatic.

Similarly, deadening of a relationship is likely if two avoidant persons leave issues unresolved for prolonged periods. Long-standing unmet needs that go unaddressed lead to resentment, chronic feelings of deprivation, and suppressed contempt. If communication doesn't improve, deep sadness and unresolved grief develop.

The habit of blocking consciousness of one's distressing emotions is likely to lead to difficulty tolerating any frank emotional experience, negative or positive, including empathy, compassion, and love.

Claiming and Reclaiming Closeness

Are people living with irrelationship doomed to lives barren of intimacy?

That's not what attachment theory or our experience with clients indicates. An "earned secure attachment"[4] can be created by allowing compassionate empathy to break down our song-and-dance routines if we're willing to explore our feelings, needs, and old ideas about relationships.

Managing many moving parts can lead to so much confusion that it may make us want to return to hiding in our song-and-dance routines. But deciding to keep the door open to learning new ways of interacting with others can be enough to start the process of building a new life.

Exercise: Reflecting on Your Own Family *(Individuals)*

Is irrelationship in your family? The following brief exercise may provide some clues.

Write down the names of people you remember who figured significantly in your life when you were a small child—caregivers, other family members, neighbors—it could be anyone. Then write reflections or even just single-word impressions you have about each person.

- What do you recall about each person that influences how you view or relate to others as an adult?
- What connections do you see between how they treated you and how you behave toward others now?
- What do you protect yourself from by keeping your distance from others?

GRAFTS: Types of Song-and-Dance Routines

Our song-and-dance routines are techniques we developed as small children to change our early caregiver's emotional state, so they were able to take care of us. Children in families where this occurs become exquisitely perceptive of other's emotional states and unspoken needs and become masters at managing other people to keep them from being angry, upset, or sad. Over time, the routine becomes ingrained and shapes our view of ourselves and everyone and everything that is part of our world. Our identity becomes organized around the need to be a caretaker and our demand that those around us align with our caretaking routines. So what does this look like in a child?

A wide variety of patterns of interaction—for which the authors have devised the acronym GRAFTS—become grafted onto a child's personality in response to her or his experience with early caregivers. The following table includes brief descriptions of the GRAFTS and why the child starts acting them out.

	Descriptors	Explanation
G	Good	We believe our caregiver needs us to be a "good" girl or boy, driving us to be good all the time with everybody.
R	Right	We're driven to do everything exactly right, hoping, and finally believing, that doing so will make our caregiver feel better. Sometimes this develops into a need to be strong or competent in all situations.
A	Absent	We believe we can help our caregivers by staying out of their way. This is often seen in children of a severely depressed parent but sometimes in children whose parents are not engaged or who have poor coping skills. The absent routine is virtually always characteristic of the Audience.
F	Funny	The child is constantly "on," looking for ways to make the caregiver laugh, thus dispelling her or his negative emotions. When we figure out what behavior is most effective as a mood changer, we make it our "first line of defense" against anxiety.
T	Tense	This adaptation is a constant state of unconscious anxiety that keeps us walking on eggshells so we don't upset our caregiver. We also avoid calling attention to our own needs or even thinking about them.
S	Smart	In households where intelligence is valued, children elicit attention by making themselves knowledgeable in areas calculated to please the caregiver. Children locked in this behavior often deprive themselves of exploring their own interests.

When we use these GRAFTS techniques and they seem to work, we learn to believe we can fix our caregivers by changing their mood, which makes us feel safer.

Exercise: GRAFTS Assessment *(Individuals)*

Do you recognize any of these GRAFTS behaviors in yourself or someone close to you? The following is a quick assessment to help you decide.

- Do you remember times you used any of the GRAFTS? Do you remember why? Explain.
- Are you aware of having continued that GRAFTS behavior as you got older? How did it change?
- Whom have you used a GRAFTS behavior for? How did they respond?

- How did you know when to use a GRAFTS behavior? Are you aware of currently using any of the GRAFTS in the following situations: workplace, friends, family, or romantic involvements? If so, why do you?
- Has using a GRAFTS behavior had an impact on your social life? Physical health? Work life and finances? Your state of mind?
- Do issues related to GRAFTS have anything to do with your choosing to work on your relationship now?

Exercise: GRAFTS Role Reversal (*Individuals*)

Each item in the GRAFTS table represents a role reversal in which a child takes on a caretaking role for the caregiver. This distortion of roles and boundaries profoundly impacts the child's feelings of safety.

In the following exercise, see if you can relate to the examples given. Consider each GRAFTS behavior, and then list ways that your own behavior had an effect on how you related or still relate to others.

Role Reversal	Who I Performed for	Impact on Me
My mother was always criticizing herself compared to other mothers, so I worked harder at school hoping she wouldn't be so down on herself.	My mother	I ended up acting like a "know-it-all" at school, which made other kids avoid me.
My parents fought a lot, but they'd stop when I'd pretend I was on stage doing a singing or comedy performance.	My parents	I made myself responsible for their relationship. Sometimes it backfired, and they'd yell at me for being silly.

Exercise: GRAFTS Family Rules (*Individuals*)

In the following exercise, list examples of how family song-and-dance routines became inflexible family rules when you were a child. Then describe how this affected you. Some examples are listed in the table.

Family Rule	This Rule Came Out of Routines Enacted with	This Rule's Impact on Me
Don't show your feelings.	Dad	When family arguments broke out, I'd leave the room, so nobody would know how afraid I was. I was left in isolation with my fear.
Always be on my best behavior outside the house, so nobody suspected anything was wrong with our family.	Mom	Since I could never just be myself, I made almost no friends in school.

GRAFTS caretaking roles can be replays of old family rules that get in the way of family members' caring for one another. These rules even enable parents to avoid responsibility for giving their children the care they need.

After reviewing the broad-brushstroke examples in the following table, list your own examples of song-and-dance routines (GRAFTS) that became inflexible rules in your relationships and describe how this affects how you connect with others.

Rule	How This Rule Plays Out in Our Relationship	How This Rule Impacts Our Relationship
Deny everything.	Instead of openly discussing troubling issues with my partner, I ignore problems and pretend everything's fine.	Even though we live together, mutually agreeing to ignore troubling issues leaves both of us feeling isolated and alone.
Blame others.	I tell my wife we have money problems because she can't get a decent-paying job.	I used my salary as justification for humiliating my wife, who already feels bad about how much she makes. This also makes her feel like she's not entitled to say anything back to me.

Note that caretaking routines are actually the opposite of showing empathy—and in fact actively get in the way of doing so. Pummeling others with caretaking makes it impossible for them to offer anything in return. This is a primary purpose of irrelationship.

Exercise: GRAFTS Roles and Rules *(Individuals and Couples)*

Revisit the GRAFTS exercises that you have already completed, identifying ways that you and your partner act out roles and rules that you remember from the household in which you grew up. After identifying your GRAFTS roles, use the examples in the following table to help you to draw out how your GRAFTS routine(s) originated and how they play out in your relationships.

Roles I Play in Our Relationship	How and Where My Role Originated	Effects of My Role on Both of Us
I often play the victim.	It's how my father responded to my mother's domineering behavior to keep the peace.	I keep my real needs hidden from my partner for fear of disturbing the peace and end up feeling neglected and abandoned.
I stick to a bystander role when anything goes wrong in our relationship.	When I was a kid, we lived with my father's parents. They constantly criticized my mom, but my father never stood up for her.	When my partner has problems with others, I silently look for ways to blame him for it.

Next identify and list the unspoken rules that have been established in your relationship. Refer to the table for examples.

Relationship Rules I've Implicitly or Explicitly Agreed to	Where I Learned These Rules	How These Rules Affect Our Relationship
We have to stay together at all costs.	My parents stayed together, even though they hated each other.	The threat of being alone is so scary that I'm afraid to reveal negative feelings to my partner for fear he'll leave me. So I pretend everything's okay.
We don't talk to each other about behavior we don't like.	My parents never argued in front of us or allowed us to argue about anything.	Discussing relationship issues is out of bounds, so I'm always tense and tiptoeing around my wife. I don't know how long I can continue this.

Learning to open up about your part in your song-and-dance routine is the beginning of creating genuine connection on which to build your shared life. You can start right now by reflecting on your experience as a couple. Describe ways that roles played out in your family of origin negatively affect your relationship or relationships now. Use the examples in the following table to get in touch with your own feelings and thoughts and get your process started.

Roles Each of Us Acts Out in Our Relationship	Origin of These Roles in Our Individual and Shared History	Effects of These Roles on Our Relationship
I'm like a cop monitoring everyone's behavior—especially my partner's. I'm always ready to pounce if he does anything I don't like. And I don't always wait until we're in private to do it.	My mother was always lying in wait for my father to do the least little thing she didn't like.	I've caused pain and created distrust that makes my partner unwilling to confide in me or go anywhere with me. He says he constantly walks on eggshells around me.
I'm always the martyr. I congratulate myself for putting others' needs ahead of my own.	My father had a stroke when I was a teenager. Mom made a point of letting everyone know about the sacrifices she made to take care of him. Meanwhile, if we kids needed anything, she said we were selfish.	People outside the family say I'm a saint, but nobody in my family even tries to talk to me since the day my husband blew up and said I'm always complaining about what I have to do for others. He doesn't even try to listen to my side of the story, and now I feel cut off from my own family.

Now describe ways that rules negatively affect your relationship. The following table may provide helpful examples.

Rules We've Implicitly or Explicitly Agreed to	Origin of These Rules in Our Individual or Shared History	Effects of These Rules on Our Relationship
Each partner is allowed to believe that what they contribute is good enough.	My older sister acted as if our parents' undependability caused no problems in our family life. But as soon as she was old enough, she left home and never looked back.	I never complain about my partner's contribution to our home life, but now I resent and feel resented by her.
We will pretend everything's fine.	My mother was terrified that the neighbors would find out about my father's drinking and the problems it created at home and on his job.	Early in our relationship, my boyfriend and I never found a way to talk about any kind of relationship or household issues for fear of creating problems. Now we barely talk to one another beyond small talk as we leave for work. Our schedules make it impossible for us to have dinner together. Sex has disappeared.

Self-Other Help Exercises

Up to this point, you've been looking at your own histories, feelings, and behaviors to see how they align with the irrelationship adaptation. Now you're going to move into learning techniques of Self-Other Help—simple tools that have the power to undo what your histories have created and open a space for living in relationship sanity.

Exercise: The Audacity of Listening (Couples)

Having explored the dynamics of irrelationship in preceding sections, the following questions will help you explore your past relationships and articulate how you'd like to change.

Begin by explaining to one another how you understand irrelationship: what it is, how it works, how it affects you, and things about yourself and your relationship that you'd like to change.

1. Share feelings about what it's like to see your interactions as self-protective devices that get in the way of growing closer to each another.

2. Talk together about what you believe you were protecting yourself from by using these devices.

3. Discuss what it might be like to be open to unpredictable feelings, especially anxiety, and what might happen if you were.

Exercise: Reflection *(Couples)*

Learning to practice open dialogue with those we're close to almost inevitably opens our eyes and ears to parts of ourselves that we may not easily become aware of otherwise. This is key to practicing compassionate empathy.

The following practice helps to disarm the tendency to get down on yourself about parts of your past that you're uneasy or embarrassed about. Reflecting directly on such experiences tends to disempower leftover anxiety or shame. This short-circuits the temptation to retreat into the familiarity and security of irrelationship.

1. Tell your partner about an experience in the past—distant or recent—that made you feel anxious, embarrassed, or guilty.

2. As you reflect aloud on that experience, deliberately try to reconnect with the discomfort it caused you.

3. Write down what it's like to return to that experience and its associated feelings.

Exercise: Approaching Compassionate Empathy *(Couples)*

Sit in silence together for one to two minutes and try to focus only on your breathing. Setting a timer may be helpful.

After the period of silence, take turns saying each of the following statements to one another.

- Blaming and punishing harms the process of getting well for both of us.
- We can help each other feel accepted and cared for.
- We can learn to feel safe enough to touch and be touched by each other.

After a pause, tell each other about feelings or memories that came up as you did this practice. Write them down, noting similarities in what came up for the two of you. Afterward, explain in writing your ideas about where this practice could lead your relationship.

Staying on Target: GRAFTS versus Relationship Sanity Assessment

Understanding your own song-and-dance routines—and how they are expressed by GRAFTS—is an essential step on the road of relationship sanity. A major aspect of your work here has to do with forming a better understanding and acceptance of yourself—your whole self with needs and desires—through your relationships with others. Song-and-dance routines are a a code that allows those invested in irrelationship to be protected from *hearing*, while *listening* is the vehicle of compassionate empathy.

Key Takeaways

- The process of receiving (accepting) and giving care that forms the foundation for relationship sanity is the best way to work through irrelationship and the key to building and maintaining healthy relationships in our life.
- Together we can build self-compassion and acceptance.
- Through this process we learn to allow life to happen without any interference.

- In this process, I will—and we will—be able to finally answer the question: What do I need?
- In this process, I will—and we will—be able to finally answer the question: What do I *really* need?

Now pause and look at each other. Use free association to discuss any thoughts or thought fragments, feelings, reflections, and analysis of where you were and where you're headed—individually and as a couple—along the road of recovery from irrelationship, the road of relationship sanity.

Chapter 3

Compassionate Empathy in Our Everyday Lives

Loneliness while in the company of another is a common symptom of irrelationship. In fact, it is often the first breakthrough symptom in those bottoming out on irrelationship.

"Of course, it makes perfect sense," Felicia said. "Dealing with loneliness isn't something I can do, well, alone."

Felicia was used to the safe busy-ness of her family and social life. She unconsciously but purposely ignored how she never talked with anyone about how she felt or what she needed.

Sharing our deep feelings cuts through isolation creating an opening for compassionate empathy, which is the way out of irrelationship. While empathy can lead to a loss of boundaries, compassionate empathy practiced jointly promotes connection that applies to oneself as much as to others, creating safety for everyone involved. This by definition undermines isolation and self-obsession.

Felicia and George are a great example of a couple who were invested in evading one another in order to avoid their own internal discomfort.

"Keeping George at a distance was such an old habit that the idea of opening up to him about my feelings was the last thing I'd have thought of doing."

Without knowing it, Felicia and George had replaced intimacy with a brittle idea of safety that excluded revealing one's vulnerability, showing feelings, or sharing experience meaningfully. In short, their relationship had become a dead space.

Felicia's finding courage to talk about her loneliness created space for George to reveal that he felt the same. It was eye opening for both of them.

"I'll ever forget the look on his face: my George—always so cool, so in control—looked like he didn't even know where he was. And then, oh, *so* relieved! The next thing I knew, he was telling me how far away *I'd* felt to *him*, how lonely he'd felt without me. *My* George telling me *that!*" She paused then continued, "I'd completely lost touch with my husband—the man I was *living with!*

"Well, all of a sudden, years of resentment I'd been carrying around just melted right then and there. And—this is so strange to tell—it was like I got a look back at how crazy I was about him when we first met!"

Compassionate empathy, the mechanics of relationship sanity, opens the way to truly being *with* another person rather than deliberately constructing your life to protect yourself from letting her or him see and know too much about you. By deliberately choosing to really hear one another with compassionate empathy, Felicia and George were able to recover the emotional connection that brought them together in the first place. Plus taking joint ownership of their positive and negative feelings, the anxiety about their family that each had suffered with in isolation for years not only became manageable but added new depth to the intimacy they were now beginning to create.

Escaping Irrelationship: Building Compassionate Empathy and Intimacy

Unlearning the old, bad habits of irrelationship doesn't happen instantaneously. Patience and persistence are vital to building the "us-ness"— the third entity that is the relationship itself—and both partners share the responsibility of maintaining its well-being. Without this mutuality, too much is demanded of one partner, giving rise to fear of loss—precisely the type of fear that creates irrelationship in the first place. The habit of compassionate empathy, however, cultivates intimacy that can be relied upon in virtually any type of crisis.

Exercise: Practicing Compassionate Empathy in Daily Life (Couples)

Irrelationship protects us from our vulnerability to people close to us by deflecting awareness of our own needs and desires. Compassionate empathy opens us up to naming and owning our feelings as well as to caring for another human being; however, compassionate empathy has to be cultivated to maintain relationship sanity.

Discuss the following questions with your partner.

- What is it like to think about the mutual openness of compassionate empathy?
- What personal implications do you think this may have for each of you right now?
- Reflecting on other relationships—past and present, romantic and otherwise—how has your *idea* of closeness affected how you connect with others?
- What thoughts do you have about how your personalities mesh with one another?
- What role does self-acceptance play in your interactions with others? What role does it have in doing this exercise together?
- What do you *feel* you need from one another?
- What thoughts and behaviors prevent you from asking for or receiving what you need? Where does this come from?

Exercise: Compassionate Empathy 1 (Couples)[1]

Place your hand over your heart, sense the warmth of your hands, the gentle pressure of your hand on your chest, and feel the rhythmic movement of your chest rising and falling with each breath.

Take a few deep, deliberate breaths, slowly exhaling each time as you visualize negative emotions draining out of your body. Then allow your breathing to naturally become normal again.

Notice whether you feel relaxed or tense without focusing on it. Just name the feeling then let it pass from your attention. This is subtle and not easy for most of us at first.

Now revisit the questions you explored previously in "Practicing Compassionate Empathy in Daily Life" to gain insight into how your feelings and perceptions have begun to alter as a result of what you've learned up to this point.

- What is it like to think about the mutual openness of compassionate empathy?
- What personal implications do you think this may have for each of you right now?
- Reflecting on other relationships—past and present, romantic and otherwise—how has your *idea* of closeness affected how you connect with others?
- What thoughts do you have about how your personalities mesh with one another?
- What role does self-acceptance play in your interactions with others? What role does it have in doing this exercise together?
- What do you *feel* that you need from one another?
- What thoughts and behaviors prevent you asking for or receiving what you need? Where does this come from?

After completing these questions, talk together—sharing and listening—about what you're feeling about one another in this moment. What is it like to talk about these feelings?

Staying on Target: Irrelationship versus Compassionate Empathy

As we said, at the end of each chapter of the book, we'll take time to reflect on your changing relationship with our song-and-dance routines and assess your progress in moving toward the *real* goal: relationship sanity.

Key Takeaways

- Relationship sanity is the practice of being genuinely *present* for each other through authentic giving and taking.
- Compassionate empathy, i.e., open-hearted listening to hear one another, is the technique underlying development of relationship sanity.
- This cannot happen without acceptance of and compassion for oneself.
- This self-acceptance is the grounding of sane interactions with those around us.
- Stumbling blocks implied by irrelationship include (1) unease with feeling compassion for oneself; (2) feeling undeserving of kindness toward myself and from others; (3) the habit of viewing one's actions and feelings judgmentally instead of gently and with acceptance; and (4) a poorly develop conception of the importance of taking care of oneself.
- Compulsive caretaking of others stands in the way of understanding and addressing these issues.

Compassionate empathy opens us to intimacy—genuinely knowing, experiencing, and caring for other human beings to whom we're drawn and vice-versa. It's a reciprocal process that makes the co-ownership of a relationship possible. Intimacy built on compassionate empathy is essentially relationship sanity. Compassionate empathy is a shared way of relating to each other in which each party gives and receives no more that 60 percent and no less 40 percent of what each brings to the table.

Now pause and look at each other. Using free association, discuss any thoughts or thought fragments, feelings, reflections, and analysis of where you've been and where you think you're headed, together, as you move from irrelationship to relationship sanity.

Chapter 4
Self-Other Help

Self-Other Help is a new paradigm distinct from the well-known self-help paradigm. The problem with self-help, for our purposes, is that working in isolation risks reinforcing isolating protective mechanisms. Moreover, relationships can't be fixed if both parties don't do the work together. Besides, research more than suggests that when we work with someone else to create positive change, whether it be exercising, improving our diet, or breaking old bad habits, we're more likely to succeed if we work with a buddy.

All this sounds hopeful, so where's the rub?

For many people affected by irrelationship, exploring what lies behind their song-and-dance routine is frightening. Fear of rejection can be real enough, but the backstory of irrelationship is usually that you find yourself living with—and defended against—someone who not only would accept you as you really are but *wants* to be close enough to know the worst things about you with no thought of cutting and running.

Dark Entries

When her mother was diagnosed with breast cancer, Mia began noticing a new distancing between she and her husband, Ethan. Somehow, this crisis was changing how they experienced their marriage.

Mia, a successful professional who believed her husband, a jazz musician, to be a diamond-in-the-rough, willingly supported his on-again-off-again music career. Ethan graciously played his part as the receptive Audience to Mia's role as Performer. As far as he knew, both of them were satisfied with this comfortable arrangement.

Mia was the couple's activities planner. Ethan generally went along with his role as the appreciative, if sometimes reluctant, participant in social activities. The only exceptions were Ethan's music gigs. Mia would preen herself on her unselfish willingness to allow Ethan to bask in the occasions when he occupied the spotlight.

Early in her life, Mia had taken on the role of emotional support for her mother, who she believed needed cheering up because her father's work kept him away from home frequently. While this didn't leave much room for Mia to pursue her own interests, it seemed to give purpose to her life.

Mia's experience with her mother arguably set her up to become Ethan's caretaker, although she insisted that taking care of him gave joy and purpose to her life and didn't feel confining in the way taking care of her mother did. In any case, the stress of her mother's illness made their emotional distance unbearable for Mia. But Ethan's family backstory made the distancing hard on him too.

Ethan's parents' constant fighting and on-again-off-again marriage made for a home life so chaotic that his brother coped by retreating into apathy while Ethan adapted by adopting the Absent GRAFTS behavior: he stayed out of sight as a small child then as he grew he stayed out of the house as much as possible. His Absent routine came to include drinking alcohol and staying out late even during the school year. By the time he was seventeen, he had a serious alcohol problem and an arrest record. His parents barely seemed to notice him most of the time, although they were forced to bail him out of jail more than once, making no secret of their concern for what the neighbors might think.

All this time, however, Ethan maintained a loving relationship with his maternal grandmother, who had never approved of his mother's marriage. At one point, grandmother and mother had a major disagreement when

Ethan's parents wouldn't allow him into the house, which left him squatting in a small apartment his rock band used for rehearsals.

One afternoon when he was at the apartment, alone and depressed, his grandmother knocked at the door.

"Ethan," she said, "I'm a little lonely there in that big house and was wondering if you'd consider coming to live with me?"

Ethan recalled the story vividly. "She saved my life. She cared for me in ways I'd never been cared for before. Suddenly, I wasn't getting drunk every day, didn't have any more run-ins with the cops, and took the band more seriously. I think it was the first time I ever really enjoyed my life. I even surprised everybody by actually graduating from high school."

Not long after graduation, his grandmother was diagnosed with terminal cancer.

"It was the worst thing that's ever happened to me," said Ethan, "but I wouldn't have missed a second of it for anything. It gave me the chance to give back what she had always given me. Sometimes it felt like I was dying too, but I was with her until the very end."

To be able to be present with Mia during her mother's illness meant Ethan would have to revisit the anguish of his grandmother's illness and death.

"Mia almost seemed to be sleepwalking when she wasn't crying, while I felt that I was stuck in one of those dreams where you can't make your voice work.

"Finally when I realized Mia was going through what I went through with my grandmother, the whole thing flipped. I was back in the head I was in when I lost my grandmother, and it hurt like hell. But Mia and I really loved each other, so I wanted to bridge the distance. I coughed and sputtered a little at first, but I knew what it was Mia needed and I showed up. And I did it."

A breakthrough of compassionate empathy broke Ethan and Mia out of years of playing Performer and Audience.

"It wasn't easy," said Ethan.

"No," agreed Mia, "but we found a way to stick around and make it happen together."

Is Dependency a Bad Word?

The path from irrelationship to relationship sanity leads through various types of dysfunctional dependency. The exercises in this chapter are designed to help you build—together—a sense of Self-Other that belies the bad rap the term *dependency* gets in our culture.

Self-Other, as a key component of relationship sanity, is built upon the bedrock of healthy interdependence[1]—which is synonymous with relationship sanity, especially as the primary goal of all attempts to work through the irrelationship defense. Self-Other is the us-ness that we—our relationship itself—form in relationship sanity.

What then does healthy interdependence look like?

Exercise: Irrelationship versus Relationship Sanity (*Individuals and Couples*)

The purpose of this exercise is to help you understand how your individual tendencies join to create an irrelationship song-and-dance routine, as well as to identify opportunities for opting for relationship sanity instead.

In irrelationship, extremes of anxiety about intimacy, both too high and too low, prevent discovery of dysfunctional relationship patterns. With relationship sanity, moderate levels of anxiety are adaptive, allowing the couple to recognize and address issues without being overwhelmed. Insufficient or suppressed anxiety mutes awareness of problems that need addressing, while excessive anxiety hampers our ability to focus on them, as illustrated in the following diagram.

Awareness of Fear of Intimacy and Health of Relationship

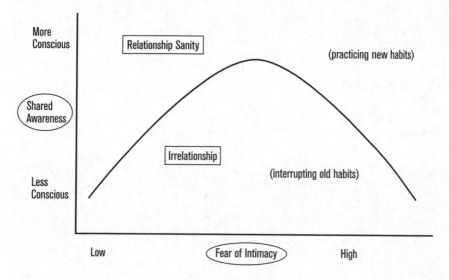

Now take some time to review the habits associated with irrelationship and relationship sanity. The subsequent table contrasts irrelationship- and relationship-sanity associated thoughts and behaviors you should consider when doing a Self-Other Assessment (40-20-40), which you will complete in the next chapter.

	Irrelationship	Relationship Sanity
Thwarting vs. Receiving	· I don't allow others to help me, fearing what it will cost me. · I don't allow others to know about my needs. · I don't accept instruction or advice. · I hide things I don't like about myself.	· I'm receptive and responsive to help offered by others. · I seek and make use of support from others. · I don't need constant care and reassurance to feel okay. · I'm able to share my anxiety and insecurity with others.
Unreliable vs. Dependable	· I have trouble staying with a task and following through on commitments—even small ones. · I avoid problems and conflicts by caving in, regardless of my feelings and opinions.	· Reliability is important to me, and I feel strongly about showing up when I say I will—even for relatively small commitments. · I have a history of being reliable and trustworthy. · I believe in the importance of persisting at finding solutions to issues that satisfy all affected parties.
Exemption vs. Accountability	· I look for ways to blame and find fault. · I hide and deny my questionable behavior. · I hide my mistakes. · I avoid taking responsibility. · I assume and tell others that their problems are their own fault and don't shy away from scapegoating.	· I take responsibility when I'm at fault. · I accept accountability for my contributions to problems and make amends when I hurt others. · I can acknowledge parts of myself that aren't as mature as I would like. · I make and keep commitments. · I can be honest about my part in conflicts.
Fear of Isolation vs. Healthy Independence	· I can't stand being alone but still feel isolated even when I'm with others. · I have a hard time setting boundaries and am hurt, confused, and frustrated when others have boundaries that seem to exclude me. · I hesitate—or don't stand up—for fear of rejection. · I am unclear about what I really think, believe, and care about. · I seek attention and approval from others in almost every area of my life.	· I'm clear about needing to be alone at times and can enjoy it. · I'm able to set boundaries, accept those set by others, and believe this to be healthy. · My ideas, opinions, and feelings are entitled to respect even when countered by others. · I am interested in knowing and furthering my sense of self. · I am comfortable with who I am.

	Irrelationship	Relationship Sanity
Passive and/ or Aggressive vs. Assertive	· I'm aggressive with others as a means of getting my needs and desires met. · I avoid overt conflict but otherwise will do anything to get my way. · I believe bullying others is acceptable to get what I want. · I don't stand up for my opinion in conflict situations. · I let others off the hook if they don't support and care for me in difficult times.	· I'm able to ask for what I need. · I do my part to ensure that my plans come to fruition. · I can engage in conflict directly to resolve differences. · I like and am engaged in my life. · I can disclose and struggle with feelings and ideas in order to invite the support of others.
Disregard/ Disdain vs. Positive Regard	· Criticism and shaming others is sometimes necessary to bring about desired ends. · I sometimes withhold opinions out of concern that others "wouldn't be able to take it." · I impose my will on others when I know what's best for them. · I believe devaluing myself and others is appropriate at times. · I believe it's often my place to fix, or rescue, others.	· I'm competent at finding ways to care for myself. · I seek and find ways to care for others. · I respect the right and need for others to find solutions to their problems but will offer help if asked. · I respect the dignity and rights of others, regardless of their emotional, psychological, spiritual, and intellectual development. · I accept and offer nurturing to others based on mutual respect and efficacy.
Self-Sufficient vs. Partnership	· I avoid helping others and don't let them help me. · I am able to work things out on my own and believe others should do the same. · My solutions are mine, and I deserve credit for them. · I pride myself on being independent and self-sufficient. · I sometimes believe it is necessary to allow others to believe they're in charge while I quietly find ways to undermine their power and take charge. · I have difficulty accepting gifts and compliments from others.	· I am willing to offer and accept help. · I am willing to offer assistance without taking charge. · Problem-solving with others is gratifying and likely to create novel, more effective solutions. · I enjoy sharing management, ownership, and leadership. · I enjoy collaborating on and implementing others' projects. · I enjoy receiving compliments and accept gifts with gratitude.

Reflect individually on the following list and write down whether and how they form part of your current relationship. Refer to the previous table as needed, but don't overthink: give the first answer that comes to mind.

- Receiving
- Thwarting
- Dependable
- Unreliable
- Accountability
- Exemption
- Healthy Independence

- Fear of Isolation
- Assertive
- Passive or Aggressive
- Positive Regard
- Disregard/Disdain
- Partnership
- Self-Sufficient

Next review your responses individually and jointly, noting similarities and differences in your patterns. Discuss the role these patterns may have in your song-and-dance routine.

Recall a specific interaction you've had together that left you feeling dissatisfied, even if it didn't result in overt conflict. Tease out concrete examples of how the interplay of your individual behaviors may have been what left you feeling uncomfortable.

Exercise: From Irrelationship to Compassionate Empathy (Individuals and Couples)

The following table contrasts interactions among people affected by irrelationship with people who integrate compassionate empathy in their functioning. Keep in mind that compassionate empathy is a *practice* rather than a *goal*.

	Irrelationship	Compassionate Empathy
Isolation vs. Showing Up	· I make a point of keeping my feelings to myself. · I avoid making myself available to others—usually because I'm afraid of what they'll think of me. · I keep my head down to avoid attention, good or bad, from others. · I have a hard time responding to others' needs. · I tend to get lost in my own head rather than being present to others.	· I can share my feelings when I believe others are interested in me. · I'm open to being available for others. · I can give and receive attention to and from significant people in my life. · I'm gratified by responding to others' needs and can communicate my desire for reciprocation. · I enjoy the presence of others as well as being present to them.
Depletion vs. Creativity	· I prefer to let others take the initiative. · I tend to stay by myself. · I feel drained or ripped off when people want something from me. · I get embarrassed and ashamed when I have to reach out to others. · I feel that most things happen to me without my being able to control them.	· I am able and willing to ask for help from others. · I can enjoy both solitude and the company of others. · Sharing tasks and resources feels empowering and energizing. · I feel that others are willing to help me when I need it. · I can share my concerns and problems with others.
Avoidance vs. Accessibility	· I instigate conflict to prevent resolution of issues—both inside and outside myself. · I avoid addressing relationship issues. · I avoid initiative or leadership roles so that I can't get blamed if anything goes wrong. · I have a lot of life issues and loose ends that never seem to get resolved.	· I prefer to see conflict situations through to resolution in order to understand the underlying issues. · I listen for my own part in conflicts, so I can contribute to the solution. · I try to remember to reflect on my feelings before I take action to avoid muddying the waters. · I'm okay with not having the answers to relationship problems and seek to solve them jointly. · I try to separate out and address problems one issue at a time.

	Irrelationship	Compassionate Empathy
Unavailability vs. Openness	· I keep my thoughts and feelings to myself. · I rarely seek advice on important decisions or even talk them out with others. · I avoid placing myself in a position where I'm expected to help others with their issues. · I maintain the appearance of being busy, so others won't try to impinge on my time.	· I try to maintain openness to others' need for care and support. · I prefer to bounce important decisions off others whose judgment or experience I respect. · I share what is going on with me when I'm confused about a problem or relationship.
Resentment vs. Generosity	· Giving or receiving empathy makes me feel anxious and drained. · Supporting others feels too risky. · Validating or complimenting others makes me afraid I'm giving away too much.	· I value empathetic exchange. · Mutual support of others is gratifying. · I can express in words and actions my appreciation for others. · I can give others negative feedback without putting them down.
Non-Acceptance vs. Acceptance	· The way I see the world tends to overcome my capacity for positive experiences and feelings toward others. · If I observe problems in situations or other people, I feel it's important for me to step up and fix them even if it's costly for me to do so. · I avoid involvement in problematic situations unless I can control the outcomes. · The prospect of change in relationships or life-situations is frightening.	· I'm able to use humor as a tool in addressing problems with others. · I accept that life isn't always to my liking but can remove myself from harmful situations. · I'm open to new ventures and projects and seeing where they will take me. · Any life experience, positive or negative, may have potential for a positive impact on my life.

As you contemplate each of the habits listed in the previous table, rate to what extent you identify them in your current relationship. Complete your reflections individually and refer back to the table as needed, and then discuss what you've found with one another. Don't overthink: give the first answer that comes to mind.

- Showing Up
- Isolation
- Creativity
- Depletion
- Accessibility
- Avoidance

- Openness
- Unavailability
- Generosity
- Resentment
- Acceptance
- Non-acceptance

Reflect together on your ratings, using the following questions to guide your discussion.

- What do your ratings suggest about how you interact together?
- How can this information be used to build greater closeness in your relationship?
- How does doing this exercise affect how you view the process of relationship building?

Exercise: Compassionate Empathy 2 *(Couples)*

The purpose of this exercise is to cultivate the ability to focus on only one thought, question, or facet of an issue at a time.

Using a timer, spend three to five minutes sitting quietly and looking into one another's eyes. Afterward, reflect together on the following questions.

1. What's it like to be quiet with someone who's important to you?
2. What's it like to consider letting that person get closer in new ways you may not be able to control?
3. What's it like to try to put aside what you're thinking and focus on what your partner is thinking or saying?
4. What's it like to watch your partner going through the same thing?

Write down your individual key reflections on this experience. Read them aloud to each other, pausing between each response to allow them to sink in.

Exercise: Compassionate Empathy 3 *(Couples)*

Using a timer, sit together quietly and practice the Joint Compassion Meditation Exercise in Chapter 1. Take care to maintain your awareness that both of you are vulnerable and uncertain but safe.

Recall things you've said to one another in the exercises up to this point. Reflect on what it's like to be sharing this experience of opening up to each other. Then imagine your partner doing the same thing—*with you.*

Bring your attention to any physical sensations of stress you've become aware of as you've proceeded through this practice.

Ask one another if you're aware of any behaviors or other markers that have surfaced in each other as you've proceeded through this practice. Discuss them.

Repeat this process to take note of any troubling emotions or feelings that have surfaced. Then share these with each other.

Staying on Target: Self-Sufficiency versus Self-Other Help

The paradigm shift from self-help to Self-Other Help occurs in the mundane—becoming the average, expectable everyday—use of compassionate empathy. Compassionate empathy allows you to make practical use of the relationship sanity you're building together and connect with intimacy compassionately. This means that you've created and are sustaining a space where both of you are giving, receiving, and accepting each other in a kind of stimulus (I give to you) response (you receive from me) manner that you can then regularly pass back and forth between each other. This opens up the space for you to experience yourselves as *us*; this us-ness is the relationship itself. It then becomes a shared responsibility to take care of the relationship—just as you take care of yourselves and each other. This can only be done consciously if you are doing it reciprocally—in compassionate empathy, that is, relationship sanity.

Key Takeaways

- We're developing a joint understanding of what it is like to be forming—in the presence of another person—the space, the feeling, and the experience of Self-Other in the heart and mind—that way we behave with and relate to someone who is significant in our lives.
- By doing this work with someone significant in our lives, we are with someone who now genuinely threatens—and provokes hope within—and there just might be ways of breaking free from the straitjacket of irrelationship, the prison cell of isolation.
- We're becoming able to address this question: What's it like to listen to and take in what someone who's important to us has to offer?
- Additionally, we're learning about other questions: What is it like to see someone we care about taking the risk of valuing what we have to offer? What's it like to be with him or her as we go through this process? What's it like to let another person see that we value him or her in this way?
- Finally, we're learning how our shut-down self-awareness has affected how we are with others: What is it like to recover our suppressed emotional investment in another person? How does that relate to how we connection with the world in general? What changes does this imply for all our relationships?

Still working toward changing your relationship and your song-and-dance routines, it's time again to assess your progress in moving toward the *real* goal: relationship sanity.

Now pause and look at each other. Use free association to discuss any thoughts or thought fragments, feelings, reflections, and analysis of where you were and where you're headed—individually and as a couple—along the road of recovery from irrelationship, the road of relationship sanity.

Chapter 5

Self-Other Assessment: The 40-20-40

The 40-20-40 establishes a safe space for partners to interact by creating a middle ground (20 percent) for negotiating issues created by differences they bring to the table from their respective (40 percent) positions. In the middle ground, we learn to accept a partner unconditionally as she or he really is and receive what she or he offers without intruding into her or his side, i.e., no further than 60 percent. At the same time, we maintain responsibility for what we bring to the table—our 40 percent. *Finger-pointing, blame, and criticism are out of place.* This leaves a 20-percent space in the *middle*—a space that is *ours*, a space for an ongoing process of developing and expanding us-ness.

The 40 percent on either side of the equation represents what we think of and experience as *our part* of a problem, conflict, issue, or solution to said conflict. The 20 percent in the middle represents shared ownership/accountability of the issue/problem/conflict at hand—ultimately of the relationship itself, the *third* thing that is an *expanding middle,* or us-ness.

Remain mindful that vulnerability doesn't go away as you move forward with this process; but sidelining blame and criticism allows both partners to be truthful and feel heard, respected, and safe. This gives us space so we can

- discover ways to manage anxiety that weren't available to us when we developed our song-and-dance routines;

75

- repair our relationship by taking gentle responsibility for our contributions to how our relationships function;
- empower ourselves by analyzing how our current style of interacting developed in our families of origin, re-awakening feelings we suppressed which we actually need to experience healthy intimacy as adults;
- use our new understanding and returning feelings to create better alternatives to stultifying irrelationship patterns;
- accept one another as we really are and enjoy greater freedom in more authentic mutuality.

In this way, couples establish joint ownership of their relationships by working together through the most frightening parts of themselves and their underlying fear of letting others know them.

Anomalous Apathy

"I always told my friends that my parents were strict, especially my mom, but that turns out not to be how it was. The truth is, she was so checked out that I did anything and everything to get her attention."

Beau's mother was a war widow—not that her husband was killed during enemy action, but he returned home addicted to heroin, similar to many Vietnam veterans. Overwhelmed by this loss, she shut down emotionally, leaving Beau feeling mystified, abandoned, and hurt. He responded by anxiety-driven attention-seeking that became increasingly mixed with anger. This led to his mother's repeatedly imposing new house rules, which only made Beau angrier.

Apathy can be a powerful impetus for creating irrelationship routines. Apathy in a child's caregiver is likely to elicit one of three types of song-and-dance routines from the child.

1. Being Good—exceptional behavior of some type, intended to awaken the attention of the caregiver.

2. Becoming Absent—keeping out of sight in order to lessen demands on the caregiver.

3. Behavior that is so unacceptable that it demands attention. This is not altogether different from the Good behavior first mentioned.

Beau's Performer routine was even more complex; however, it was not just a way of getting attention. He used it to distract his mother from the severe depression she developed when her marriage ended. In short, Beau became his caregiver's caretaker.

Reverse Caregiving

A relationship that steers wide of awareness or expression of one's own needs or desires is a subtle caretaking routine—one that Beau and his mother shared. Keeping feelings under wraps provided both with camouflage for Beau's dangerous drug use, which he developed as a teenager. He had a particularly dramatic run-in with the police on a Friday night when he was twenty years old and was working at a court-imposed community service job. The following Monday, he expected to be terminated and sent before the judge again. Strangely, his mother seemed unaffected, and the court didn't take any notice.

"What's going on here?" Beau thought.

In reality, this was just another in a long series of drug-related incidents spanning nearly a decade, the consequences of which never quite seemed to catch up with him. As for Beau's depressed mother, she kept herself ignorant of Beau's more outlandish behaviors as a survival strategy for herself. This strangely made Beau feel even more mystified and angrier. They were actually colluding at not-knowing about one another's feelings and needs.

"Everybody I knew was getting in real trouble over drugs—why not me?" Beau reflected. "I told myself that all my mom's rules just showed how controlling she was and was just waiting for me to step out of line. When she didn't even ask about that arrest and I didn't get fired from the job, everything I told myself about the world just kinda fell apart."

In a way, Beau's experience was reminiscent of Slavoj Žižek's quip that finding out your partner's having an affair is bad enough, but even worse is your partner finding out you're having an affair and not caring.[1]

Beau brought his song-and-dance routines into relationships with girls and women as he got older. Overwhelming them with his unending performances, he left little room for them—or anyone else—to show any real interest in him, much less love and caring. For Beau, this translated into apathy, an absence of any real feeling for him, which drove him to even more extravagant behaviors and performances. At the same time, he was unable to show caring for others, much less expose any sort of emotional vulnerability, except from behind the wall of his song-and-dance routines. And his perpetually being up in that way carried the added benefit of conveying that he wasn't vulnerable, didn't need anyone, and could survive without anyone's regard or care.

"Always getting away with it left me in a dark place like I was the only one alive in a world of zombies. I had no idea how to bridge the distance."

A Self-Other Assessment using the 40-20-40 establishes that middle ground between ourselves and our environment, making it the cornerstone of relationship sanity.

Exercise: Roadblocks to the 40-20-40 *(Couples)*

Many of us deliberately avoid exploring what our part is in the problem areas of our lives, especially in significant relationships. This exercise helps you practice exploring those problem areas.

With your partner, agree on a relationship problem or issue you have—recent or ongoing—that you're willing to explore. Then write down feelings and reflections you have about *your individual part* in that issue.

Next discuss the following questions, focusing on *your part* while keeping in mind that finger-pointing and criticism are out of bounds.

- How did you initially understand the issue?
- What was it like to write down your part in the issue? Has doing so caused anything to shift in how you see it?

- How do your own negative feelings, such as shame, anger, or fear, get in the way of your communicating honestly with others?
- Has the issue included perceived injury? Retaliation? Recurring arguments? What is the outcome of these?
- Have either of you threatened to end the relationship? What brings this about?

Implementing the 40-20-40

The 40-20-40 can be used virtually anytime, anywhere—even in public places. It can even operate powerfully as a spot-check inventory when a couple is confronted with a highly charged situation that threatens to get ugly fast. When each party maintains focus on her- or himself, this is likely to defuse an acute crisis, allowing more balanced communication to resume or replace the agitated state.

The following describes the basic structure and ground rules for using the 40-20-40.

- Shares are best when strictly timed. Five minutes are suggested for each party's initial share and then three minutes for each share thereafter.
- Interruptions and arguments are out of bounds.
- Both parties may share only what they are feeling but must be able to do so without fear of blame, criticism, or having what they say used against them during the 40-20-40 *or at a later time*.
- Each party must be able to safely acknowledge his or her part in what's happening, both good and bad.
- Both parties listen to *hear* what is being said without blame or criticism in order to improve mutual understanding.
- The parties take turns sharing until they feel that at least a temporary, workable resolution has been reached.

How the 40-20-40 Works

First Half   **Second Half**

Person A Speaks   Person B Speaks
Person B Listens   Person A Listens

Speaking   -------------------------------------> Listening
 ↓ ↑   ↓ ↑
Listening   <------------------------------------- Speaking

It may sound daunting because it's so different from how we habitually communicate. However, be patient with yourself and each other: most of us aren't in the habit of sharing feelings and needs honestly and are bound to make mistakes as we learn how to do so. But with practice, the anxiety that stands in the way of open and honest communication begins to fade as well as our need for our bad, old habits.

Since irrelationship has, in a manner of speaking, worked for a long time, our song-and-dance routines can be hard to give up; however, the honest, effective communication that takes its place is likely to be so gratifying that we'll much prefer dancing together to dancing around one another.

The 40-20-40 isn't about keeping score: it's about listening to and learning from one another in ways that probably excited us when we first met yet frightened us as the possibility of intimacy loomed closer. This new willingness to find our way back to one another is the essence of relationship sanity.

Exercise: Identifying Positive Experiences (Couples)

Recall an experience you shared early in your relationship that seemed to carry a lot of promise for your future together. It may be a trip you took, finding a home, or making a major purchase together.

Next describe the experience for one another, including how it felt to be doing it together. Then write down two or three aspects of the experience that you felt made it important to your relationship.

Exercise: Asset Mapping *(Individuals)*

During this exercise, you will consider how specific personal attributes affect your relationships. First in each section, you will list your assets that play important roles in how your relationships function. Then you will list traits that need improvement or are otherwise problematic. Finally you will reflect on traits and techniques that may be useful for approaching relationship sanity.

Capacities, Gifts, and Skills
1. What attributes do you recognize in yourself that are consistent with relationship sanity? How have you used them to improve the quality of intimate or other relationships?
2. How have you failed to use these attributes in intimate or other relationships? What was the effect of not doing so?
3. How might items that you listed in "Capacities, Gifts, and Skills" Question 1 be used to lessen the impact of items in Question 2?

Commitment
1. How have you shown willingness to be accountable for your part in relationship issues?
2. How have you avoided accountability for your role in relationship issues or conflicts?
3. How might items that you listed in "Commitment" Question 1 be used to lessen the impact of items in Question 2?

Authenticity
1. In which ways are you consciously able to open yourself to others, especially those closest to you?

2. What behaviors do you use to avoid intimate exchanges with others, for example, placating, denying or minimizing problems, etc.?

3. How might items that you listed in "Authenticity" Question 1 be used to lessen the impact of items in Question 2?

Alliance

1. In which ways do you consciously make yourself available to others in order to share tasks or solve problems?

2. What techniques do you use to keep yourself apart to avoid sharing tasks with others for fear of getting too close?

3. How might items that you listed in "Alliance" Question 1 be used to lessen the impact of items in Question 2?

Meeting Needs

1. How do you let others know you need their assistance in meeting your needs? What things do you do for yourself to meet your needs?

2. What behaviors and habits do you have that prevent others from knowing about your needs or helping you to meet them? How, in your ideas and actions, do you prevent self-care that would help you meet your own needs?

3. How might items that you listed in "Meeting Needs" Question 1 be used to lessen the impact of items in Question 2?

Decision-Making

1. When faced with an important decision, what actions do you take to reduce anxiety around the issue and make the best decision you can?

2. What behaviors do you use to avoid difficult decisions and choices? Are you aware you're doing it when it's happening?

3. How might items that you listed in "Decision-Making" Question 1 be used to lessen the impact of items in Question 2?

Emotional Openness

1. In which circumstances and situations do you feel safe sharing your feelings with others?
2. Which circumstances and situations make you feel uneasy or unwilling to share feelings?
3. How might items that you listed in "Emotional Openness" Question 1 be used to lessen the impact of items in Question 2?

Following Through

1. What resources and support do you need to help you follow through on decisions and commitments?
2. What has interfered with your willingness and ability to resolve unfinished business and follow through on decisions and commitments?
3. How might items that you listed in "Following Through" Question 1 be used to lessen the impact of items in Question 2?

Exercise: Asset Mapping *(Couples)*

Having taken a look at your assets and how they can be used to create relationship sanity, take a look at assets of your relationship itself apart from your individual traits.

Similar to the previous exercise, you will record your relationship's assets or strengths in the first part. Then you will list characteristics of the relationship that could use improvement in the second part. Finally you will reflect on how you can improve upon the items you listed and record any thoughts or ideas in connection with undertaking this process as a couple.

Sharing

1. How do we maintain balance in giving and receiving? What makes this meaningful and satisfying?

2. What interferes with our ability to share with one another? What relationship experiences are unsatisfying or leave negative feelings behind?

3. How could we work together to use items that we listed in "Sharing" Question 1 to improve on items in Question 2?

Fellowship

1. How do we, as a couple, welcome others into our shared life and seek support when we need it?

2. Which mechanisms do we use to keep us isolated from one another and from others as a couple?

3. How could we work together to use items that we listed in "Fellowship" Question 1 to improve on items in Question 2?

Conflict Resolution

1. When we've had relationship conflict, which techniques have we used to deal with it that have left us feeling satisfied with the outcome?

2. Which avoidance behaviors (or words) do we use to skirt around conflict thus leaving it unresolved?

3. How could we work together to use items that we listed in "Conflict Resolution" Question 1 to improve on items in Question 2?

Crisis Management

1. When serious crises have arisen in our relationship, what did we do to get through them that left us feeling good about the outcome?

2. Which behaviors do we perform or share that prevent us from working constructively through crises?

3. How could we work together to use items that we listed in "Crisis Management" Question 1 to improve on items in Question 2?

Stress Regulation

1. What do we do to manage stress so that it doesn't escalate into conflict or crisis?

2. Which shared behaviors do we use to avoid dealing with stress?

3. How could we work together to use items that we listed in "Stress Regulation" Question 1 to improve on items in Question 2?

Intimacy

1. Which words and behaviors do we use to communicate that we accept and are committed to one another unconditionally?

2. Which behaviors or mechanisms do we share that allow us to avoid exposing ourselves to the risk of rejection?

3. How could we work together to use items that we listed in "Intimacy" Question 1 to improve on items in Question 2?

Boundaries

1. Which words and behaviors do we use to indicate mutual respect for healthy boundaries?

2. Which words, behaviors, or incidents in our history indicate that we haven't resolved the issue of personal boundaries versus sharing and intimacy?

3. How could we work together to use items that we listed in "Boundaries" Question 1 to improve on items in Question 2?

Acceptance

1. When have we been able to discuss each other's negative traits with one another? Give examples.

2. When have we avoided discussing negative traits or experiences with one another for fear of rejection? Give examples.

3. How could we work together to use items that we listed in "Acceptance" Question 1 to improve on items in Question 2?

Sharing the information uncovered or discussed in these exercises can be a watershed in relationships marked by the denied or inexplicable distance of irrelationship. Having become accustomed to the standstill over time, the thought of disturbing it can arouse anxiety. But exercises like the previous ones lead a couple through a process of exposing their vulnerability together, which goes a long way toward defusing that anxiety.

Exercise: Sharing Compassionate Empathy (Couples)

The following practice helps couples build and expand safety and intimacy with one another by exploring compassionate empathy.

Set a timer and spend three to five minutes facing one another, sitting comfortably and quietly. Let yourselves become conscious of what it's like to be here with your partner.

Next intentionally try to get a sense of what this experience is like for your partner to be here with you, especially the emotions she or he may be experiencing.

Now imagine what your partner would say to describe what it's like to be here with you.

Reflect together on the following questions.

- What's it like to think about accepting your partner *exactly as she or he is?*
- How can we agree to show up for one another without trespassing into each other's 40 percent of the 40-20-40?
- What would it be like to commit to this agreement unconditionally?
- What would it be like to tell your partner about your needs?
- What would it be like to have your partner tell you about her or his needs?
- What do we notice about one another as we reflect on these questions or techniques?

Staying on Target: Us versus You and Me

As you build your alliance as partners, you have seen how you can use the 40-20-40 to co-create a safe space wherein you can feel that, yes, there is you, and yes, of course, there is me, but in this 40-20-40 space there is a third thing: *us!* Now you can feel that us-ness as a middle ground for negotiating issues created by differences that you each bring to the table. In the middle ground, you learn to accept a partner unconditionally as she or he really is and what she or he offers without intruding into her or his side. At the same time, you maintain responsibility for what you bring to the table—your 40 percent. *Finger-pointing, blame, and criticism are out of place.* This leaves a 20 percent space in the *middle*—a space that is *ours*, a space for an ongoing process of developing and expanding us-ness.

Key Takeaways

- We have a shared, consensual, and practical answer to the question: How can I accept what the other person has to offer?
- We know how to work through any and all resistance to those things that irrelationship protected us from: empathy, intimacy, vulnerability, and emotional investment. With the insight we have gained together through this awareness, we can now answer the question: How can I commit to giving no less than 40 percent and no more than 60 percent and be accountable/responsible for the health and well-being of our relationship in similar measure?
- We have a willingness to be a part of a whole, which we have developed and now maintain together. In this us-ness, we can now ask and answer the following questions.
    - o How can we help each other?
    - o What do we need from each other?
    - o What do I need from you?
    - o What do you need from me?

o What can we do to more consciously be aware of our concerns and anxieties so as not to slip back into our old—and effective—ways of protecting ourselves from interpersonal anxiety?

When you allow yourselves to both care for and accept care from each other—using the 40-20-40—you can be peaceful in larger settings, bringing the compassionate empathy and sense of interpersonal safety and security with you wherever you go.

Working through your characteristic ways of cutting yourself off from accepting what others have to offer, to give through the 40-20-40, allows you to more fully, more consciously, accept yourself and others in your life, as well as the conditions in your larger and ever-expanding life—as they actually are.

Now pause and look at each other. Use free association to discuss any thoughts or thought fragments, feelings, reflections, and analysis of where you were and where you're headed—individually and as a couple—along the road of recovery from irrelationship, the road of relationship sanity.

Chapter 6

The 40-20-40: Relationship Sanity in Action

Nurturing a middle ground in which differences with those around us can be negotiated is necessary for relationship sanity. This work is done jointly by the invested parties who are willing to learn to communicate honestly and effectively with each other.

A nemesis of relationship sanity is the Credit-Blame Syndrome. The Credit-Blame Syndrome uses a lot of finger-pointing—some verbal, some not—but never really meets anyone's needs or solves problems. Dismantling irrelationship, then, isn't about learning how to be fair when placing blame: it's about examining how our life choices have stood in the way of meeting our real needs.

How will you know when your investment in irrelationship is diminishing? The answer is that you'll know—you'll feel it—when what you give in your relationships feels balanced with what you receive back from your partner.

The 40-20-40 Model of Relationship

So how does the 40-20-40 help address this situation?

Imagine that you and your partner are sitting in chairs at a table ten-feet wide. A line bisects the table at the exact midpoint, leaving five feet between each of you and the midpoint—ten feet apart. Imagine a line in the exact midpoint between you—a 50-percent line. That leaves five feet between each of you and the middle.

You	Mid-Point	Me
0 Feet	5 Feet	10 Feet
0%	50%	100%

Next imagine expanding the width of the line in the middle of the table so that it occupies an area that's 20 percent of the width of the table, leaving 40 percent on each side of the midline for each of you.

You		Expanded Middle		Me
0 Feet		4 Feet	6 Feet	10 Feet
	40%	20%	40%	

This model illustrates a reciprocal dynamic between two people. If responsibility for what goes right and what goes wrong in relationships could be split evenly, balancing giving and receiving in relationships would be simple. However, everyone coming to a relationship brings histories, traits, needs, and desires, making the balancing process complicated and messy even for those who do have insight into what they bring to the table. In other words, a relationship is always more complicated than the sum of its parts.

The 40-20-40 is a Self-Other Assessment in which the parties examine individually and jointly the part each plays in the relationship and the effect her or his contributions have on each other and the sum. Each party may take no more than 60 percent and no less than 40 percent responsibility for any given issue. This leaves a 20-percent space for a couple to meet in the middle where they can safely articulate their issues and experience without blaming. This allows nonjudgmental validation of each other's experience, placing the couple on a better footing for mutual understanding and shared problem solving.

Gettin' the Band Back Together

Tyrone shared his experience of finding out that the 40-20-40 can work with others besides intimate partners.

"Janelle and I had been using the 40-20-40 for a while when a major battle of wills began to shape up in my band. Then it hit me: maybe guys are so wrapped up in their own issues that, for whatever reason, they just can't hear each other. So I thought, 'What about the 40-20-40?'"

Irrelationship roles can develop between virtually anyone in any situation in which a person is invested but feels vulnerable and at risk.

"The band had busted up over and over again—usually with a lot of drama. But nobody was talking about their own feelings: we'd just blast one another when we got pissed off. And sometimes it was obvious we weren't blasting somebody that we had a real issue with. It seemed like a perfect situation to try getting the guys to look at what's really going on instead of just getting mad and getting out."

Tyrone's band wasn't just a bunch of kids jamming together in somebody's garage: they had high-level name recognition in their area of the country and had even been heard and approached by a scout from Los Angeles. But their on-again-off-again relationship not only put the band's name recognition but also their finances in jeopardy—something their manager repeatedly warned them about.

"Things were a real mess at that point. One of the guys was especially ticked off at our manager. We had to do something if we weren't going to blow up past the point of no return. So I told the guys, including our manager, how the 40-20-40 worked. At first they were kind of unsure about it but finally agreed to give it a try.

"From the start it reminded me of me and my wife: the singer was always acting like he's doing us a favor by just showing up—usually late—but nobody ever called him on it. The bass player made it no secret that he was always auditioning for other bands—or saying he was going to. Our drummer always stayed out of everything—kept in the background and never said jack shit, no matter how pissed off anybody got about anything, including his mistakes.

"But the weirdest thing was a couple years ago when our sax player died—OD'd on heroin. I'm telling you, *everybody* loved this guy; but, suddenly, there we were dead in the water, like for months. After his memorial, people started missing rehearsals—had other things they had to do or they just didn't show up. But we never talked about it—just like we didn't talk about Ronnie dying, and we never looked for another sax player.

"And then our manager! Jeez! You'd think he was our mother, constantly bugging us about how we spent our money, what we did with our time—and I mean our *free* time! We had this laundry list of messed up stuff, and everybody was walking around like everything was cool.

"Well, it took some doing, but I got everybody to agree to meet at a diner we went to sometimes, and I explained the 40-20-40 to them—said I thought we had a lot of stuff we needed to work on and told them how it had helped Janelle and me. And they knew that was for real because they all knew something had happened that had really changed our marriage. So anyway, bottom line, they were willing to give it a try.

"I explained the ground rules, and one of us kept the stopwatch. And it was hard at first because everybody had all this stuff going on with themselves and about the band. But the funniest thing was that when we started sharing, every single one of us admitted we were afraid to say what was on our mind because we were afraid of saying something that would *ruin the band!*

"The hardest part for everybody was talking about what was going on without blaming somebody, or, the flipside, without somebody feeling attacked when they really weren't. That's what goes on in the real world too:

everybody's so into their own image that you just instinctively say, 'I'm cool, I've got this.' Well, we finally got to where we were all able to say that we *weren't* cool, or we *didn't* know what was up or how to handle it. In fact, I think the best thing for the band has been learning to trust each other like that. It makes you feel like you're part of something *real.*

"And, man, it's deep sometimes. I remember when Jorge was still pretty new to the band, and he was badmouthing our manager one time. But instead of getting mad, our manager called a 40-20-40! And what happened? Jorge, the new guy, admits that he's insecure playing with us—doesn't know if he's a strong enough artist. And he was looking over his shoulder, waiting for our manager to tell him he didn't make the cut. Well, this was all because our manager never said anything to Jorge about his playing. And that was where we all got to help him out because our manager never says anything about *anybody's* playing. But how could Jorge know that? He just took it personally. So we got to tell him that we *all* had stories about our manager, which totally changed everything. Funny thing is, after that, Jorge's playing went off the charts!

"One of the biggest things to come out of this is that we love playing together and we love saying so to each other. Of course we have our issues, but nobody's afraid somebody's gonna blow up the band if we talk about it. In the past, we acted like a bunch of martyrs, keeping all that stuff to ourselves. And then, when Ronnie died, we felt sucker-punched, but nobody felt like he could bring it up. And I gotta tell you, when that was going on, our rehearsals were horrible. It felt like nothing was ever going to be right again.

"Well, it's not like that anymore: if something's bothering somebody, we can't give it a pass because we care about each other; and anyway, it affects how we play. So if we need a 40-20-40, we stop rehearsal and have a 40-20-40."

Exercise: Practicing the 40-20-40 (Couples)

Revisit the Joint Compassion Meditation in Chapter 1 before proceeding to the 40-20-40 practice with your partner.

Previous exercises lay the groundwork for the next exercise by creating a safe space for risk-taking. The 40-20-40 allows couples (or larger groups) to hit pause when conflict occurs to provide an opportunity for identifying and addressing problems jointly. Begin your practice by doing the following.

- Identify an issue or disagreement in which each party is willing to discuss her or his part.
- For agreed upon time-intervals, each partner take turns describing her or his own part, positive and negative, in the issue. Start with an opening exchange of five minutes each, with a series of three follow-up exchanges of three minutes per person. As you proceed, take note of feelings and thoughts your partner reveals that you identify with and share these in your next turn to share. After completing four exchanges, assess the 40-20-40.

Remember that the purpose of this practice is not to identify points of criticism or blame but to promote taking co-ownership of your relationship. But go easy on yourselves: most of us require practice to learn to remain within one's own 60-percent zone.

Use the categories listed here to assess your practice of the 40-20-40, looking for strengths and areas you can improve. As you consider the following table, which shows each dimension of relationship sanity on a spectrum from low to high, make note of whether you more strongly identify with the items on the left compared with the items on the right.

Irrelationship ⸻⸻⟶ **Relationship Sanity**

Compassionate Empathy	
I felt distance between what I thought and what my partner experienced. I felt criticized and unheard. I felt uneasy and unsure about reaching my partner.	Listening to and hearing one another felt natural and wasn't confused by my own feelings. The practice felt "caring" and like an opportunity to learn from each other.

Interdependence	
I feel that I'm better able to manage my life without disturbances like this. We have so many problems that we'd probably be better off on our own.	Though we have problems, I feel that sharing like this strengthens us and makes our lives better.

Independence	
The 40-20-40 Exercise highlighted that our relationship doesn't help me feel less anxious or isolated.	The 40-20-40 Exercise promoted acceptance of differences without disturbing my appreciation for my partner.

Now imagine a relationship where you no longer need to play the good, right, absent, funny, smart, or tense caretaker by either Performing caretaking routines or playing appreciative Audience to ineffective care. This is an in-between space—a space between irrelationship and relationship sanity to be filled in with compassionate empathy before it regresses. Consider the following questions.

- Being released from your role, who are you now?
- Who have you become? Who are you becoming?
- How does this change feel frightening or bad (e.g., "I'm a bad person because I am selfish and too expressive of my own needs.")?
- And how does this change feel like a relief or otherwise good (e.g., "I feel compassion toward my significant other but I understand that it isn't helpful for me to suppress my own needs until I am ready to burst.")?

- How has acting the part of the Performer/Audience made you suffer or feel anxiety or anger, and how do you feel about seeking peace and joy in the future?
- How has acting the part of the Performer/Audience made the other person suffer or feel anxiety or anger, and how will you think about this in the future, so you can be more active and engaged, still a great listener, but not disengaged in unhealthy ways?

Take five to ten minutes to reflect on this experience. If you are feeling distressed, consider hitting pause to think, feel, and reflect. Afterward do something *for yourself* to practice the behavior of accepting and receiving something positive, even soothing, for yourself—generosity, kindness, gentleness. Remind yourself that, in the past, you and your partner have used our compulsive caregiving song-and-dance routines to block yourselves from accepting and receiving.

Then discuss the following questions with your partner.

- What aspects of practicing the 40-20-40 seemed to go well?
- What was difficult about it?
- What would you like to do differently next time?

Staying on Target: The Blame Game versus the 40-20-40

Research shows that harsh self-criticism undermines motivation, while compassion promotes motivation. Together, you can use the co-creating of compassionate empathy to help establish a new way of relating that fosters the development of the capacity for discernment: the ability to see and appraise oneself through the expanded experience of Self-Other Help.

Allowing yourselves to receive kindness and balance, you can put yourselves into mutuality with others and recognize that the trap of destructive self-criticism has been used as an unconscious defense from opening up to the care—acceptance—of others. By opening up to Self-Other experience, you can cultivate an appreciation and affection. You can develop a way of relatedness characterized by encouragement and support and by understanding where things went the wrong way and making the necessary course corrections without getting mired in traps of self-sufficiency, i.e., isolation.

Key Takeaways

- We co-create ways to make practical use of the 40-20-40 Model, as implemented together via the Self-Other Assessment (and in groups via Group Process Empowerment) that allows us (or all in the case of groups) to (1) address an issue, conflict, or problem together or (2) hit pause and then consider our own contribution—good, bad, and in-between—to the issue at hand.

- We understand how to establish a safe space for each of us to begin to take risks, take personal inventory—our own and not each other's—and care for the developing relationship sanity that is replacing irrelationship.

- We consider ways in which self-criticism can be replaced by compassionate empathy and how this—like a new pair of glasses—supports an experience of Self-Other, empowerment, and discernment as a way to feel safe. It can be an effort to

  a. keep from making the same mistakes over and over again;

  b. become a real collaborator in partnership with real people defending themselves from intimacy;

  c. better understand our part in current interpersonal dilemmas and make good with people we may have offended;

  d. keep a connection going with loved ones from the entirety of our history by recognizing that opportunities for working through historic conflicts will play out with significant people in our current lives—that irrelationship will rear its head in the relationships that threaten us with intimacy now.

Now it's time to pause again and assess your progress in moving toward the *real* goal: relationship sanity. In that pause, stop and give yourself time for free-association. Write down any thoughts or thought fragments, feelings, reflections, and analysis of where you were and where you're headed—individually and as a couple—along the road of recovery from irrelationship. Then discuss between yourselves.

Chapter 7

Practical Applications of Compassionate Empathy

Projecting the appearance of intimacy facilitates avoiding serious issues. Occasionally, however, a crisis may force an opportunity on us for breaking through the tidiness we project to one another.

You Scratch Your Back and I'll Scratch Mine

"Everybody knows money issues hammer a lot of relationships," Ravi remarked. "But a big fight over what we owed the IRS hammered ours back together."

Worrying about one's image can be used to justify withholding important information from one's spouse or partner. We may even tell ourselves we're doing it to protect her or him; however, it usually has more to do with fear of telling the truth about something we've done that troubles us.

Ravi was a successful hedge fund manager who made some poor finance-related decisions that he kept from his wife, Kamala. While Kamala sensed something was wrong, she ignored the feeling for fear that she'd learn about something she didn't want to know. Their choices delayed a major opportunity for creating deeper intimacy in their marriage.

"Kamala and I both came from loving homes in which making a lot of money wasn't a high priority. My parents were proud that I planned to study engineering in the States and go back to India to work for the government. But when I got to New York, the guys I hung out with—mostly other guys from India—convinced me to switch to the MBA program since math was so easy for me. And what happened was incredible: even before I graduated, Wall Street firms were all over me. It was very heady. And sure enough, within weeks of taking my first job, money was flowing in and out so fast that, before long, I stopped paying much attention to how much I was making compared to how much I was spending."

"I have to admit, it was very exciting," Kamala put in. "I never thought my life could be like that."

"Before long," Ravi continued, "I got into this kind of competitive thing with other guys—the expensive clothes, the watches, the cars—and using credit cards like there was no such thing as credit limits or APRs. I know I went months without even looking at my statements."

"Yeah, me too," Kamala chimed in.

"The problem is that I got so careless that I didn't think about the IRS. Other guys bragged about how their lawyers kept them out of trouble with the IRS. So when the IRS first came knocking, I figured—well, I don't know what I figured and I definitely didn't tell Kamala about it. I guess I figured my tax accountant would work it out without Kamala having to know anything about it. And anyway, it was *my* money that *I* earned, right?

"Well, my lawyer was emailing me, left messages, and even sent me a registered letter that the warnings from the IRS were getting serious. Well, the way I handled it was still not telling Kamala anything about it, but I *did* start to get pissed off about how much she was spending. But the truth is I never actually *said* anything about it to her—not about our bills, our spending, and definitely not about the IRS.

"Then one day my accountant sent me copies of IRS correspondence that made it pretty clear that I was looking at prison for felony tax evasion if we didn't do something, and fast. He also let me know that his firm, which prided itself on being squeaky-clean, was starting to give him a hard time for continuing to carry me as a client."

Meanwhile, Kamala, still in the dark, was becoming increasingly worried that something was wrong and Ravi was keeping it from her.

"Ravi started coming home after he knew I'd be asleep. And he always had something he had to do related to business, even on weekends. When I *did* see him before work, I could almost always tell that he'd been drinking late the night before because I could smell it. Usually, though, we hardly saw one another for weeks at a time.

"At first I made excuses for him. I told myself he was so busy because the market was bad. Anyway, that's what everybody said, so I played along," Kamala admitted. "I pretty much just ignored the way he was avoiding me. I even wondered if he was having an affair, though I never really believed it. We've been in love since before college, and our sex life was always great—or had been. No—I decided it had to have something to do with his work.

"Well, when Ravi finally told me he was in trouble with the IRS, I was shocked—blindsided—but relieved in a way, actually, because it meant our marriage was okay. Or so I thought. But the more I thought about it the more it hurt that he never told me—that he obviously didn't think he could confide in me.

"Just when I was trying to explain that to him, it hit me: When I was pretending all those months that nothing was wrong, I was doing exactly the same thing to Ravi that Ravi did to me—and for the same reason—fear. I was afraid of what he'd think if I told him how uneasy I was becoming. In India, women are expected to leave all that sort of thing—the money, the bills—to the husband. It's practically taboo to ask questions of a man about things like that."

Ravi agreed, though his spin was even more personal.

"I didn't know what to do. I hated not being straight up with Kamala, but I was afraid she'd leave me if she knew the truth. So instead of going home after work, I went out drinking. And I hated myself for it. Protecting Kamala was the worst thing I could have done—to her, to me, and to our marriage."

A Bridge Back to Love

Carol's marriage to Vanessa was the perfect hiding place. For years, she carefully managed the image of an orderly relationship and household.

"It was sealed up tight. All anybody knew about us was that I always kept my cool. Nobody suspected—least of all me—that I had no idea how to be there for another person, especially Vanessa. I didn't even know what that meant.

"When her mom's Alzheimer's got worse, I may as well have been invisible. I had no clue what I could do to help Vanessa get through it and wasn't about to ask."

Keeping her emotional distance was how Carol had managed her own mother's death four years earlier.

"I didn't want sympathy, compassion, none of it—not that I knew what any of that really was. I was going to be a tower of strength in the middle of everybody else's sadness. Vanessa tried to be there for me. She always waited up for me when I went to the hospital. But I ignored—pretended it was nothing special—that she was always up late. So I'd go to bed immediately telling her I had to do this or that for Mom in the morning—whatever, to prevent Vanessa from knowing I was actually *feeling* anything. Nope. Nobody was going to know how afraid I was of losing my mom.

"At first, it seemed legitimate. Vanessa's mom never hid her homophobia, while my mom loved Vanessa—always remembered her birthday or our anniversary. No way could you compare losing my mom to losing hers. So I pretended she couldn't possibly be suffering the way I had—or told myself I had. Well, as it turned out, keeping the whole thing at arm's length had nothing to do with how angry I was at Vanessa's mom: it was a hedge around the pain of losing my own mom. And somehow I knew that if I validated Vanessa's pain, it was going to bring me face-to-face with my own.

"Strangely, that became the moment of truth: I suddenly could see that keeping my feelings shut down was killing our marriage. If it was going to be saved, I'd have to go back to my mom's death and bring up, *myself,* what that had felt—still felt—like for me. It was the only way I could be useful to

Vanessa. Up to that moment, I'd never had even an inkling of what intimacy actually is *and* does."

Compassionate empathy allows two or more individuals to safely share each other's experiences, especially highly charged emotional issues and problems. This creates a sense of joint ownership of whatever happens in their relationship without danger to either party. If a couple steps away from practicing compassionate empathy, they run the risk of losing one another to the isolation of irrelationship.

Exercise: Constructive Conflict *(Couples)*

Recall a disagreement you had with your partner that escalated from a minor disagreement to an ugly scene in which you said things to one another that have been hard to forgive—perhaps so hard that you still haven't recovered. Write an account of the incident together.

Brainstorm together how this argument might have turned out if you had done a better job of listening to one another, trying not to retaliate regardless of how you felt about each other's position. You may like to write down some notes on points you both make. Then complete a 40-20-40 to treat the issue or issues underlying this conflict.

Exercise: Acceptance *(Couples)*

Taking in what another person has to offer—giving *and* receiving with compassionate empathy—is the heart of relationship sanity. By contrast, irrelationship is a silent distancing—even rejection—designed to conceal what we need and care about both from ourselves and from one another.

Using the following list, reach into your past and assess what you and your partner have contributed to and sought from your song-and-dance routine and what you may have lost by investing in it.

- Feelings of safety and security
- Relationships with friends, colleagues, or romantic partners who you believed accepted you as you are
- Shared life-experience

Practicing this simple type of honesty and accountability with one another creates a safe space for you to learn how to build intimacy with one another.

Staying on Target: Making Use of Irrelationship versus Making Use of Compassionate Empathy

Listening is the essence of compassionate empathy and Self-Other experience, as well as the heart of relationship sanity.

Irrelationship deflects our attention from our feelings for one another while compassionate empathy excavates our capacity to care by exposing how we've derailed ourselves into isolation as a defense against the anxiety connected with intimacy.

Key Takeaways

- We have developed a willingness and an ability to go back as far as we can in our histories to ask ourselves what each of us gained by our investment in irrelationship, for example:
    - a sense of safety;
    - a sense of security;
    - the experience of having friends, colleagues, or romantic partners who I believed accepted me as I am;
    - the experience of believing that those around me accepted and cared for me as is;
    - the experience of believing that I was good, right, absent, funny, smart and/or tense as a part of my personality rather than as a defensive/protective routine.
- Similarly, we have developed a willingness to also go back as far as we can, to ask ourselves questions about "the cost" of irrelationship, for example:
    - living in resentment;

- o thinking that I've been "ripped-off" but not knowing exactly how, when or why;
- o questioning the ways that people valued and/or accepted my contributions (caretaking) to them and their lives;
- o "feeling" a vague sense of loneliness and isolation.
- We see how our attempts to be close to others backfire in ways that we did not understand.
- We've gained essential insights that set us up to practice compassionate empathy through our willingness to find out what's *really* going on with each other and to affirm in one another the courage it takes to explore whatever we find out about each other.
- We've begun to see and feel how it "takes two to tango."
- We began to understand how we jointly created both the benefits and the costs of irrelationship.

From this point, it's easier and more useful for each member of a relationship to take stock of their situation and choices, past and present, in order to account for their own part. But remember that the purpose of this process isn't to place blame: it's so each partner can understand her or his power in interpersonal relations so that he or she can contribute meaningfully to resolving issues. This type of honesty and accountability is the framework of Self-Other experience and creating a safe space for building intimacy.

Take a moment to look into one another's eyes. Then imagine the following for some time.

- What would it be like to replace our anxiety and anger-driven song-and-dance routine with closeness and trust?
- Where might that lead us?

Chapter 8

Performer and Audience: How It Works

In childhood, both the Performer and the Audience felt acutely unsafe when their primary caregiver was in a negative emotional state. Thus they became caretakers of their caregivers by contriving patterns of behavior intended to make the caregiver feel better, which allowed them to feel safe again. Carried into adulthood, these patterns of behavior become the individual's song-and-dance routine.

The Performer gives until the caregiver feels well enough to take care of her or him. The Audience, by contrast, takes by passively appearing to benefit from the caregiver's ineffective caregiving. This reduces the caregiver's distress, allowing her or him to feel better about her- or himself.

Fear, then, drives both Performer and Audience, who, as small children, believed that if they didn't intervene, the caretaker wouldn't be able to care for them. As Performer and Audience mature, these patterns are brought into adulthood, resulting in the inability to make themselves available for genuine connection and intimacy with others.

In many cases, a person may act out different roles with different people, depending on the part the other person plays in her or his life. So don't be surprised if you find yourself identifying sometimes with the Performer and other times with the Audience: in both cases, a role is being acted out to reduce anxiety in relationships with important people in your life.

Exercise: Adult Caretaker Responses to Stressful Life Events (Individuals)

In the following table, there are two examples of common, stressful life situations that are often disruptive to relationships. Reading left to right, each example shows the response of a caretaker involved in such a situation and the consequences it has for that individual. Review your own history for similar experiences and recall examples of your own in which a negative life experience resulted in loss of investment in, or even abandonment of, a relationship.

Stressful Event that Made You Feel Out of Control	How Did You Respond?	Outcome
Loss of job	I became caretaker, assuming all financial responsibility.	I felt resentful, hurt, and unappreciated. Investment in my relationship diminished.
Financial problems	When I had money problems, I refused to let anyone else know or help.	I left relationships because I was embarrassed or I blamed myself for our poor financial state.

Exercise: Joint Responses to Stressful Life Events (Couples)

The following table gives two examples of stressful situations representing significant relationship crises. Using these examples as a guide, identify similarly stressful experiences from your own life that you believe may have created distancing or even isolation between you and your partner.

Stressful Event that Made You Both Feel Out of Control	How Did You Respond?	Outcome
Illness	We each devised individual modes of coping with the illness rather than sharing the experience and supporting one another.	Each party ended up feeling more isolated from the other.
Death of a loved one	We avoided discussing but adopted behaviors toward each other to make each other feel better without actually asking about or paying attention to what the other was actually experiencing.	Increased isolation and anger toward one another occurred as a result of not sharing and validating each other's experience.

Using the examples in the table, agree on a stressful life-event that impacted your relationship and together answer the following questions.

- How long ago did the situation develop?
- What else was going on at the time—either for you as individuals or as a couple?
- Did other life-circumstances affect your response to this situation?
- Have you been able to resolve it? If the crisis remains unresolved, refer again to the previous table to improve your understanding of the conflict.

The upcoming exercises will help you cut through what's preventing the situation's resolution. But first, take note of the following.

- Couples invested in irrelationship take actions toward one another during stressful situations that *ignore actual needs*, which increases the distance between them.
- If this pattern continues unaltered over a prolonged period, a breaking point is likely to be reached. The outcome will probably be either that (a) the partners will walk away from the relationship in frustration; or (b) one or the other or both will explode in anger as a result of neglected needs.

- Such an explosion (if it occurs) is actually a hopeful sign because it signals the persistence of genuine investment in the relationship and a desire to engage rather than isolate and ignore problems. In other words, an angry outburst may be the beginning of relationship sanity. In some cases, the explosion will be used as an excuse to bail, leaving either or both parties free to blame the other for failure of the relationship. In that case, of course, neither party is likely to have learned anything about relationship building through honest and open communication of feelings and needs.

Exercise: Exploring the Influence of Historical Relationship Patterns—Then & Now (Individuals)

The following table provides two examples of negative behavior children witness in caregivers and the resulting negative outcome that experience creates in the child's life as an adult. After reviewing the two examples, look back on your own history for points of identification or cite other examples from your own childhood in which you were negatively affected by family relational patterns.

Relationship Patterns and Behaviors I Saw as a Child	People in My Family Who Were Involved in These Patterns and Behaviors	What Effects Did and/ or Do These Patterns and Behaviors Have on Me Now?
My parents were constantly fighting with each other, but no matter how ugly it got, they always told me how lucky I was to have two parents.	My parents	I tolerate nasty behavior in others, especially people I'm involved with romantically, but I never say anything about how it makes me feel. This increases distance and resentment.
My dad complained constantly to us kids about how difficult my mom was, but I never saw him and mom try to work out a problem calmly.	My father	I stew in resentments toward others. I don't know how to approach an issue calmly to resolve it. If I ever discuss my relationships with others, it's only to complain about them.

Using the previous table, consider the ways that relationship patterns that you witnessed as a child play out in how you interact with others now—especially with people whom you have been or would be involved romantically.

Consider a relevant, past or current relational pattern that you recognize and answer the following questions.

- What effect is this pattern having on your relationships with others?
- Where does this come from?
- What other factors exacerbate how this pattern affects your interactions with others?

If this pattern is creating distance between you and people you'd like to know better (romantically or in other ways) use the previous table to get a better sense of what the pattern "looks like," and brainstorm on ways you and that person might use what you've learned so far to break through the barrier and develop improved ways of relating to others.

Stuck in the Song-and-Dance

Sometimes what appears beneficial—the "feel-good" parts of doing the song-and-dance—are so compelling that getting out of the routine isn't nearly as appealing as staying in it. If you are the Performer it is pretty heady to be told by others that you're like a mind reader; you seem to know what they're feeling even before they do. Who wouldn't like being described glowingly as selflessly sensitive to others and always willing to ensure that the needs of others are met? It sometimes feels like a full-time job, but the payoff is great, right? The Performer gets praise and admiration for always making sure someone else feels better.

And wouldn't it be wonderful, the Audience thinks, to find "the one who understands" you? The partner who is so crazy about you that he's continually anticipating your needs and taking care of them, sometimes almost before you are aware of them? He always has solutions and is so much fun to be with, smart, funny, and helpful too. When you're with him, you feel alive and full of hope and everything is going to be "right." He'll take care of you and won't hurt you—forever. And all you have to do is be yourself! Yes, sometimes it does feels a little bit as if you're exhausted or that he's perhaps too quick to tell you what your needs and shortcomings are, but nobody's perfect. He's just so helpful—without ever having to be asked.

So if it's all so good, why is your so-called relationship falling apart? Come to think of it, are you sensing a little déjà vu? You've been here before, and each time your promising relationships crashed and burned. In the beginning, when everything was perfect, each of you knew your expected part in the duet and seemed to be excited about it. So what was the signal—who said or did what—that made one or the other or both of you sense danger and cause anxiety to skyrocket? Has your irrelationship gotten a little shaky? Are there chinks in the armor? Maybe you are ready to shake it up, stop the madness, and engage in a new kind of authentic connection.

Let's take a look at what that might be like.

Working Through Different Ideas About Being Together

Amy's therapist was exasperated with his client's resistance to seeing what happened in her marriages as being attributable in any way to her own actions or choices.

"Yeah what-evs," Amy hit back, as she often did when her therapist tried to get her to look at her own behavior.

Amy, a thirty-four-year-old Latina from New York's Lower East Side, was the youngest of five children. Her parents separated shortly after she was born, after which her father moved to the West Coast and basically disappeared from her life. She was a conspicuous high-achiever who earned her MBA from a public university in New York City.

A relentless Performer, Amy became depressed and mystified as her marriage to Tom fell apart, despite how she competently did all that she did for him. Troubled by self-doubt, she was driven into therapy to try to figure out how her being so good turned out so bad. The explanation she settled on was that she had made a mistake in marrying a guy whose view of sex roles made him unable to live with a woman who was smart and competent.

Almost immediately upon meeting Paul, Amy felt he'd be a better partner than Tom, and, with little hesitation, she left him with high expectations of making a success of a relationship with Paul, whose retiring, passive demeanor led Amy to believe that he would gladly trust her intelligence, experience, and life-management skills. With this mindset in place, she felt she could practically guarantee Paul's satisfaction with his end of the bargain. Paul, however, proved not to be quite the type of Audience she expected.

After four years with Paul, Amy began to figure out that maybe Tom had really loved her but wasn't able to stomach her need to control everything—how they spent their time off, when they made love and where, or even how much he was permitted to use his credit cards. Finally, he fled the marriage. But Paul seemed neither resentful of Amy's need to control nor willing to be cajoled into her performance shtick. No matter how much she tried to elicit effusive appreciation "of all I do," Paul remained uninterested in any routine other than her presence in his life. For Amy, however, this was both unsatisfactory and unintelligible—at times even felt like rejection.

"If Paul would just *do* something, *anything*, to show me he cares," she complained.

Paul's reticence was actually a low-intensity defense against Amy's invasive routine. After four years of marriage, he felt frustrated because he had not found a way to communicate the secret he harbored: he was simply in love with Amy, and it had nothing to do with her Performer routine. Amy did not understand, and Paul understood only imperfectly that they had no space in which he—in which both of them—could safely reveal their desire to be with each other and the vulnerability that comes with revealing such desire. So instead, Paul remained passively engaged—Amy called it "moving like a glacier"—and hoped that a time would come in which he could show himself to her without driving her away or otherwise ruining everything.

Meanwhile, in therapy, Amy came to realize that a lack of presence to one another had been a crucial, missing piece that prevented negotiation and change in her marriage to Tom. Was it merely ironic and coincidental that she was now making the same complaint about Paul?

It was staring her right in the face. Was she ready to acknowledge it?

Putting into action the insight gained in therapy usually requires willingness, time, and practice. Fortunately, Amy's initial "yeah what-evs" reaction proved less durable than Paul's patience and desire to be with her. Moved by the recognition of a real need for change, Amy began to grasp that Paul's steady, if unexcitable, presence in her life was something other than disinterest: his glacial pace was his way of doing his part to catalyze a space in which they could share the work of relationship sanity.

Presence in Action

By accepting the realization and the unfolding *presence* of herself and her second husband, Amy (at first without being aware of it) was finally willing (and increasingly able) to take her husband's hand and break out of her routine.

These two—as Performer and Audience—had formerly been ships in the night—passing each other without really touching—for the majority of their time together. They finally—through that realization that led to actual presence—both showed up to be present with each other in the same relationship at the same time. Through compassionate empathy, both were released from what had been an isolating self-sufficiency throughout the history of their romantic lives and were free to love and accept each other, now, for who each *really* was.

Whereas their conversation prior to this realization—prior to establishing presence together—had been strained and stilted, there was now a flow that seemed possible when two people were in the same room (i.e., relationship) at the same time. In fact, Amy could now see how her conversations with Paul had been repetitions of conversations, or non-conversations, that she'd had with her first husband, Tom.

Those conversations barely bear repeating—they were all one-sided and were basically a series of criticisms and sometimes even verbal attacks launched by Amy in frustration over whichever husband's refusal to participate in any part of what she claimed to be the spontaneity (planning dinners, outings, trips), the thoughtfulness (buying gifts, reaching out—phone calls, emails, text messages), or the intimacy (beyond a certain point, this included talking) of the relationship.

Amy: You never (fill in the blank), Tom. You always (fill in the blanks), Paul. (No, that was not a Freudian slip; it's just that Amy's routine from one husband to the next could not be distinguished.)

Paul/Tom: I don't understand, Amy, what is it that you actually want from me?

Amy: My GOD! Why don't you listen? I keep telling you over and over again—how can you not know, after all this time, what I want? You're just like everyone else, you don't care, not at all.

Paul/Tom: That is just not true.

The blanks are filled with instructions and accusations that always prevented anyone else from actually becoming important to Amy. However, after the "what-evs" incident (as they call it), Amy and Paul now feel that their relationship is something they own and build together.

Paul: Honestly, Amy, I just don't know how we were living like that? I was so frustrated, I knew that I loved you, but I felt like there was just no way to get that point across—at least, it didn't feel like there was a way to get that point across in a way that you could hear.

Amy: I know, it is amazing how righteous I felt—I knew, then, that if you would just listen to me, if you would just do it *right*, that we would be okay. Thank goodness that's not what happened.

Paul: Sometimes I just don't really get it—why we were so distant? What really happened that allowed us to break through and reach each other?

Amy: I realized that I was not going to ever be able to hear you, Paul, not unless I could really hear myself being so distant and cold—and, what made it even worse, was that I had to face that I'd not only closed myself off from you—from us— but that I'd been doing that in all my relationships for my entire life.

Paul: I'm just so grateful that we pulled this off.

Amy: Me, too!

Song-and-Dance Routine Interrupted

It's time for a big change. Yes it's time to give up your old reliable song- and-dance routine. Enough is enough. The unlived life is painful, but it's not easy to let go of your most reliable defender against a frightening world that you can't control. And yet it is possible for life to become a satisfying combination of vitality and vulnerability.

Irrelationship is not the solution, obviously, but you've been there and now you are feeling a little suspicious, if not disillusioned, with the way you've been behaving. And that's good news because it means you haven't completely caved or given up. Your true feelings and needs are making themselves known. The cracks in your veneer are telling you that the artificial sanctuary you've purchased isn't as safe as you thought. But the cracks are also reminding you that vital parts of you, including love, hatred, fear, rage, and joy haven't gone away.

Change of this type is more rewarding than a simple awareness of denied or hidden feelings. Mutually collaborative relationships in which both parties feel safe talking about their emotions may seem terrifying— and it is, at first. But once the awkwardness and reticence are gone, things actually feel good—and right. Rather than buying off feelings because of the fear that they can't be controlled, exploring those feelings together becomes the beginning of true intimacy and exploring true possibilities.

It's time to review which role you play in the song-and-dance routine. You'll know who you are. Be honest and try not to be too self-critical. You became the Performer or the Audience quite innocently so many years ago. You will find your way out: transformative tips and practices are on the way. Challenging and then changing the way irrelationship has affected you offers an opportunity to find new paths to joy and creativity. Your willingness to move forward opens the door to undiscovered parts of yourself, new patterns of collaborating with others, and the joy of accepting life's surprising vitality.

The following irrelationship equation illustrates how the pieces of irrelationship can be useful for locating oneself in the complexity of a song-and-dance routine.

Irrelationship Roles, Characteristics, and Outcomes

PERFORMER
Gives until it hurts
Characteristics: Builds resentment, acting out of anxiety, relational imbalance, feelings of superiority, isolation, and false safety

+

AUDIENCE
Takes until it hurts
Characteristics: Impenetrability, acting out of anxiety, pretending that caretaking is effective; sabotaging efforts at caretaking (e.g. fixing, helping, curing).

=

Neither Giving
(e.g., high-level anxiety joined to habitual devaluing of the other)
Nor Getting
(e.g., solidly defended against giving or contribution by the other)

=

Emotional distance or absence protects from awareness of the anxiety associated with intimacy, emotional risk, emotional investment, and vulnerability.

RESULT
Dissociation, Isolation, Depression = IRRELATIONSHIP

Exercise: Are You the Performer? *(Individuals)*

As an adult, the Performer presents as a do-gooder or rescuer whose compulsive song-and-dance routine often includes one or more of the following:

- attempts to change the caregiver;
- attempts to change oneself;
- letting the caregiver off the hook for poor caregiving—usually by avoidance; may blame her- or himself for the caregiver's negative feelings;
- ignoring key personal or interpersonal issues and rejects anyone calling attention to them.

The following questions can help you decide if you fit the Performer role.

1. Do you find yourself doing for others because no one else will? What kinds of things?
2. Are you the one who always seems to be picking up the slack in your relationships, your household, or where you work? Give examples.
3. Does doing for others sometimes leave you with negative feelings about yourself or others? Give examples.
4. Do you sometimes get angry because things you do for others aren't appreciated or reciprocated appropriately?
5. When your partner seems unhappy, does it make you uneasy? Is this feeling genuine or is it part of a role that you act out?[1]
6. Are you able to connect feelings and behaviors in your adult relationships with events from your childhood? Give examples.
7. Do you remember your mother or other caretaker giving you responsibility for tasks directed at making your homelife safer or more stable? Give examples and describe how you responded.
8. Do you remember times when, as a child, you were expected to be a caretaker for others around you?
9. Do you sometimes feel that you had better distance yourself from people—even people you like?

10. Have you ever felt you had to do something to make people realize your good qualities? Give an example and describe how it worked out.

11. Do you and others think you are competent?

12. Do you have difficulty getting support from others when you need it?

13. Have you been blamed unfairly for problems in relationships? Do you sometimes go along to get along?

14. Have you ever had to leave a relationship because you disagreed or were uncomfortable with something going on in the relationship?

15. Do your romantic relationships tend to build rapidly and end suddenly? What do you think makes this happen?

Exercise: Are You the Audience? *(Individuals)*

Performers have a knack for zeroing in on others' vulnerabilities to find connections that feel safe and comfortable. This talent extends to knowing almost automatically how to fit their song-and-dance routine to their audience. This below-the-radar routine allows Performer and Audience to interact in a way that doesn't involve hazardous self-disclosure and intimacy. While the Performer's actions seem more candid, outgoing, and dramatic, the Audience role is equally powerful as a driver of irrelationship.

The following questions can help you analyze whether your attitudes and behaviors fit the Audience role.

1. Looking back at your childhood, do you remember times when the care you received wasn't what you needed? Do you remember being afraid to ask for anything because you were afraid of rocking the boat?

2. Do you expect your intimate partner to be someone who will take care of you? Have you been in relationships that failed because you didn't receive the care you needed?

3. Do those who are close to you become disturbed or agitated when you're unhappy?

4. Do others seem to treat you like a child? Are you uneasy about confronting this for fear they'll leave you?

5. Do you like the feeling of being taken care of early in a relationship but become tired and resentful of it later?

6. Do you expect your relationships to end in disappointment and failure and prepare yourself for it?

7. Do you recognize any of your behaviors in adult relationships as carryovers from your childhood? Give examples.

8. Do you remember acting as if your parents were good parents even when they weren't in order to avoid rocking the boat? Do you sometimes let others believe they're right, so you don't lose the relationship? Give examples.

9. Do you find yourself pleasing your partner by acting as if he or she is doing a good job taking care of you when he or she is not? Can you describe?

10. Does care and attention you receive from others sometimes make you feel uneasy or uncomfortable?

11. In your relationships, have you felt that your partner takes away your autonomy? How? How do you respond?

12. Have you ever felt that the care given by someone close to you isolates you from others? What feelings has that created in you? [2]

Performer or Audience?

Relationships that are mutual and reciprocal are unknown territory for many of us. Having learned something about the Performer and Audience roles, you can deliberately start learning to create a shared space in which issues long ignored can be addressed safely.

Exercise: Looking Back (Couples)

The following exercise is a practice for identifying irrelationship patterns and trying out communication techniques that can undo them.

- Identify what seems to be an irrelationship-based impasse in which you are both invested.
- Using the Performer-Audience paradigm, examine its pieces. Who does what in your interactions around this issue and why? What feelings does this situation create in each of you? What is the payoff?
- On the basis of what you've learned so far, imagine an alternative to how you manage this situation in real life. In that alternative scenario, what would each of you do differently? Speculate on how the alternative scenario would affect you individually and as a couple.

Next, use the following questions to improve your insight into this situation and how it plays out.

- What is going on in your relationship that makes it seem necessary to back away and protect yourself in this situation?
- What would it be like to try to work out this issue without making self-protection the first priority?
- What feelings toward your partner come up for you as you work on sharing honestly about your part in relationship issues?
- What is it like for you to hear your partner discussing what it's like to go through a difficult issue with you?
- What would it be like to use an exercise like this for managing relationship issues?

The willingness even to attempt speaking honestly to your partner about how you're feeling about difficult issues is a giant step toward intimacy, even if, at the same time, you're afraid of what will happen if you do.

Staying on Target: Song-and-Dance Routines versus Feeling

As small children, both the Performer and the Audience learned to fear that they would not be safe if they didn't do something to fix their caretaker.

No matter how many times this strategy failed to work, they remained stuck in their song-and-dance routines, enacting what learning theorists call the "sunk cost fallacy;"[3] that is, they refused to abandon their caretaking routines precisely because of how much they've already invested in it. For them, moving into Self-Other terrain is terrifying because it threatens to, and does, shatter their assumptions about the world, leaving them with their own feelings.

To be with your feelings is to be in touch with the world inside and around you and is, in fact, the alternative to acting out.[4] Irrelationship's Performer and Audience roles protect you from doing just that. While, in a way, this may seem like a rip-off, it didn't happen by accident: this dissociation is a survival technique for managing unacceptable emotions, especially fear, pain, isolation, and the trauma related to feeling defenseless and alone in a hostile world. So be gentle with yourselves as you find your way out of these roles and routines.

Key Takeaways

- We've identified the roles—Performer and Audience—that we play in our irrelationship song-and-dance routine.
- We explored the roles so we can take more steps on the road of relationship sanity.

Now pause and look each other in the eyes for a moment. Then, using free association, discuss any thoughts or thought fragments, feelings, reflections, and analysis of where you were and where you're headed along the road of recovery from irrelationship to relationship sanity.

Part Two

The Way of Relationship Sanity: The DREAM Sequence

Chapter 9

The DREAM Sequence: The Technique of Relationship Sanity

The DREAM Sequence is a recipe for recovery from irrelationship. The acronym DREAM—Discovery, Repair, Empowerment, Alternatives, and Mutuality—represents a practical technique for disentangling irrelationship and creating authentic partnership with others. By learning new ways to manage anxiety, we clear space for creating safe, intimate relationships despite our feelings of vulnerability.

The DREAM Sequence	
Step 1 **DISCOVERY**	· Hitting bottom and recognizing that you're both invested in irrelationship. · Understanding when feelings of anxiety and isolation break through and overwhelm the superficial calm of the irrelationship defense system. · Beginning to realize that irrelationship is no longer working, prompting openness to change.

The DREAM Sequence, continued	
Step 2 REPAIR	· Recognizing how irrelationship affects you as an individual. · Overcoming repression of feelings and resistance to change. · Viewing and practicing connecting with your partner as a repair process. · Viewing and using conflicts and issues as opportunities for learning how to repair relationship problems together and seeing this as the foundation of a sane relationship. · Gaining insight into how damaging it is to hide from connection and realizing that changing this is possible and desirable. · Understanding how you have refused to accept what others offer you and how this has stood in the way of intimacy. · Learning to manage anxiety by being truthful about it. · Letting go of the idea that somebody has to be blamed.
Step 3 EMPOWERMENT	· Improving self-understanding and acceptance. · Describing and developing insight into your personal song-and-dance routine and how it has stood in the way of self-knowledge. · Accepting accountability for your part—good and bad—in your relationships.
Step 4 ALTERNATIVES	· Realizing that change in your thoughts and feelings about life and other people is possible and desirable. · Letting go of the idea or feeling that relationships must somehow be controlled. · Making the Self-Other Assessment and the 40-20-40 automatic go-to techniques for dealing with anxiety, anger, and conflict. · Beginning to see and initiate concrete changes in your behavior related to how you are with others. · Cultivating the vision and desire for change and growth.
Step 5 MUTUALITY	· Forming real partnerships with loved ones. · Embracing the vitality, unpredictability, and even the downsides of life as it comes to you. · Becoming increasingly excited by the sharing of relationships in which neither party is calling all the shots. · Building a free flow of giving and receiving into your relationship, even in times of crisis and being able to acknowledge the need for help and offer and accept it. · Making the Self-Other Assessment part of daily living, sharing, and accountability. · Continuing growth as individuals and as collaborators in relationships.

The DREAM Sequence can be visualized as layers of a structure, each built upon the other. However, if each layer isn't maintained properly, the structure won't be sound and is at risk of collapsing. In this sense, the DREAM Sequence is what psychologists refer to as a developmental model whose stages, though sequential, blend and overlap. As we move forward, we remain open to learning more about earlier stages and revisit them as necessary. For example, we are likely to Discover more about our song-and-dance routines as we develop Alternatives that are part of relationship sanity.

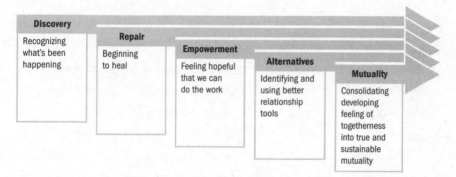

Let's take an in-depth look at the experience of two couples mired in dramatically different types of irrelationship routines to show how the DREAM Sequence works.

Patient Zero Couple

Our first book, *Irrelationship*, looked in-depth at Vicky and Glen, both psychoanalysts, whose marriage ended in a strangely undramatic divorce after they declined to confront their shared psychological defense system.

Their relationship and marriage seemed to go okay until it suddenly didn't. Although they enjoyed what appeared to others as an exciting shared professional life, for Glen, the real gratification of their marriage came from his role as Vicky's caretaker.

"It was strangely exciting to return home after I'd been out of town even if it was only for an overnight. I knew she was always going to be waiting for me to get home to help her get through something that was bothering her.

Or she'd be feeling lost or just down but knew that when I got back I was going to make her feel better. And the fact is, I liked it because it meant that she needed me."

Glen had spent most of his childhood years creating song-and-dance routines intended to make his mother feel better after her marriage to Glen's father ended after he returned from Vietnam. She was left with Glen, then five years old, whom she felt was the only part of her life over that she had any control.

But she didn't need to: Glen was totally involved in trying to relieve her depression—in later years, he referred to himself as his mother's "human antidepressant"—by contorting himself in any way he could to relieve her unhappy moods. The GRAFTS behaviors became such a pervasive part of his life that by the time he reached adulthood, they were a fundamental dynamic in virtually all of his relationships. In particular, he used GRAFTS techniques as a stand-in for intimacy when he made any attempts at romance.

"It was just how I was," Glen reflected. "Being a caretaker was what I did, so, yeah, it was even how I approached my wife—is probably why I *chose* my wife."

Vicky's song-and-dance routine couldn't have been more different from Glen's. Her ultimately estranged mother and father were so wrapped up in their anger with one another that parenting Vicky was, for them, largely an afterthought. Vicky's response was to keep herself as safe as she could by keeping out of the way of their violent arguments. Vicky's GRAFT choice of being Absent allowed her parents not to worry about whether Vicky was okay and reassured them that their marginal caregiving was sufficient for Vicky's needs.

The development of a professional crisis that overflowed into his emotional health gobsmacked Glen into realizing what kind of bargain he had made by marrying Vicky. When he turned to her for emotional support, she was unprepared and unwilling even to be present as an intimate partner and caregiver. In fact, she regarded his asking her to assume that role for him, who was supposed to be *her* caregiver, as a betrayal. After attempting to process what had and had not happened, Vicky informed Glen that he had better make new living arrangements for himself, and, no, she was *not* interested in pursuing relationship counseling.

Bracing as this scenario was, Vicky's coolness created no new emotional crisis for Glen, even though nothing seemed particularly wrong in their marriage before that. Little reflection was required for either partner to conclude that they had no interest in attempting to rescue their essentially extinct marriage or question the desirability of divorce.

The difference in Vicky and Glen's backgrounds was a setup for irrelationship. Both had histories of assuming a caretaking role toward primary caregivers: Glen by outlandish performance routines to cheer his mother up and Vicky by making herself invisible in order to avoid adding pressure to her parents' volatile relationship as well as to escape the risk they might feel if called upon to intrude into her life.

The ease with which Vicky walked away from their marriage compelled Glen to confront why he had basically chosen to marry a missing person. This placed him on the threshold of Discovery of his irrelationship routine that he'd learned as a child to protect himself from the frightening parts of getting close to another person: intimacy, vulnerability, and emotional investment.

The challenge of putting Discovery into action was put into sharp focus by the excitement he felt when he met Mai two years after his divorce from Vicky.

"When Mai and I met, I was done for—and fast! My heart was pounding—I never knew it could feel like that. It was like those silly cartoons with hearts floating around somebody's head."

Mai said something similar. "My head was swimming, but I was excited and scared at the same time."

Glen added, "I'd always made sure I was in the driver's seat with my girlfriends but knew almost right away that wasn't happening this time."

Mai's history wasn't entirely unlike Vicky's: she was raised in a small Japanese town by stern but unengaged parents whose own relationship was, at best, distant. The childcare they provided would probably be considered negligent by Westerners. Like Vicky, Mai responded to the inadequate caregiving by taking on an Absent routine: she passively accepted what her parents offered without demanding anything else of them.

However, Mai's situation was made worse by her paternal grandmother, who lived with the family and was unremittingly abusive to Mai's mother. Being born with a congenital spinal defect only made the old lady's abuse even worse; as she viewed Mai's misfortune as proof of the shame and ill fortune her daughter's marriage had brought on the family. As she got older, Mai's caretaking of her mother increased, but it was ineffective. This made Mai angry at her impotence, which ultimately became contempt for herself. Her only option, she felt, was escape.

"I had to get out but I had to make my mom and dad think that I'd be okay, so they wouldn't worry about me or think they should come to Tokyo to make sure I was all right."

Arriving in Tokyo at eighteen, Mai brought with her an almost blinding rage. Soon she was acting out with drugs and alcohol almost daily. She eventually connected with a circle of criminals so dangerous that after being in Tokyo for only a few months, she was forced to flee to the United States. After a stay with family members in California, which gave her time to take stock of her life, she moved to New York and enrolled in college. She did so well that she was accepted by a premier school of social work where she earned her graduate degree and took a job with an agency that served homeless women with severe psychiatric illness. Within a year, she met Glen through an online dating site.

Their first year together was one of unalloyed infatuation. Glen couldn't help believing he and Mai had broken the unhealthy patterns that had defined their lives up to that point, while Mai scoffed at the idea that the dysfunction of her earlier life could have an impact on her connection with Glen.

After eighteen months together, Mai thrilled Glen by announcing she was pregnant. However, just after their daughter Kumiko was born, Mai was diagnosed with thyroid cancer. Soon after, a deal to sell their apartment fell through after they'd signed a lease on another apartment. The confluence of these two issues with the arrival of a new baby created a crisis that exposed how wrong they'd been to believe they'd left old life patterns behind. Glen's reflex was to take up his old routine of feel-good performances to relieve both the pressure of their threatened financial security and Mai's self-hatred, which surfaced in her post-partum period and was aggravated by her inability to contribute financially to the household.

Glen shrewdly sized up the three sides to the crisis: (1) his own reflexive resumption of his caretaker role; (2) Mai's feelings of impotence in the face of her thyroid disease and lack of confidence as a new mother; and (3) the shared crisis of a potentially life-threatening disease and providing a suitable home for their family. Fortunately they both realized they were staring irrelationship in the face and they'd have to find their way out together.

The DREAM Sequence and Relationship Sanity

Mai's not very confidently assumed new maternal role and her health crisis primed Glen, the quintessential Performer, to offer—or, more correctly, to impose—his song-and-dance routine on Mai when her old self-hatred surfaced. Without reflecting much on it, Glen expected Mai to be the willingly recumbent Audience to his frantic, feel-better performance. That, however, isn't what happened at all.

Discovery

"I thought I hated him," admitted Mai. "Everything seemed to be going so bad, and all I wanted to do was go back to Japan. I had this crazy idea that even my mother and father would be better than this."

"I was done too," agreed Glen. "I'd done everything I could think of to fix the mess and try and get Mai to work through it. But between her thyroid and the new baby, she was in no mood to listen. I was so frustrated, so angry, that finally all I could think to say was the D word—divorce!"

Discovery is so tricky and tenuous that it can break down at any point if both parties aren't committed to sticking with it, no matter what.

"Even though I already *knew* how I used my Performer routine to push people away and thought those days were over, it kicked in when I couldn't control what was going on with Mai, the same or worse than ever before."

"Yeah," Mai agreed. "All our promises to each other went right out the window—when I found myself, in disbelief, throwing things at you."

Perhaps more dramatically, Mai ran away to Japan twice during that dark period.

"The second time I went I was sure I had killed everything. On the way to the airport, I remember thinking, 'I'm going back to Japan where I did exactly the same thing before: ruined everything for everybody when I was born.' But at the same time, I knew I was making a fool of myself and almost told the taxi driver to turn around and go back to Manhattan."

"Yeah," Glen said. "Even though I felt pretty self-righteous at first, it didn't take long before I began to feel that the whole thing was my fault. I knew—brilliant psychoanalyst that I told myself I was—that I should have known better and should have done better. That's why that day after you left, I was online looking for the first flight I could get to Tokyo."

"I didn't sleep a wink on that plane—for twenty hours I alternated between torturing myself and imaging punishing you. Then, when I got to your mom and dad's and the first thing you said to me was that *you'd* ruined everything the same way you did when you were born, oh God—I was done. What was left of my self-righteous anger melted right then and there. And anyway, I already knew way too much about what a jerk I could be to let you keep blaming yourself. No—we'd obviously made a mess of it together and we were just gonna have to fix it together."

After they had a little time to make peace with each other, Glen shared with Mai how the GRAFTS of irrelationship work and how he had become invested in his Funny and Good roles from the GRAFTS behaviors. In almost no time, Mai was able to see how she'd played Audience to Glen's Performer—mostly by using an Absent routine. And soon she'd figured out how being Glen's audience was an echo of how she'd related to her mother almost all her life.

Naming one's routine begins clearing space for compassionate empathy to enable a couple to redefine their relationship without any need or desire for hiding or finger-pointing.

"I'd always felt unlovable. So I kept up my performance routines, which didn't give anybody a chance to reject me," Glen reflected. "I *made* people like me by being funny and friendly. It was a game of perpetual seduction without ever letting anybody see how afraid I was that they wouldn't like me."

"I'd always known better than to ask for anything," Mai explained. "I learned that before I even went to school. Whatever came my way I just accepted, no matter how good or how bad it was for me. I never even thought in terms of what I actually *wanted*. That's what it was like with that stereotypical 'bad boy' I was involved with in Tokyo. Then, when it began to get dangerous, I just ran. Talk about Absent! I called my aunt in San Francisco then I packed a bag and was gone without telling anybody anything. I didn't even tell my parents until I was in California."

Repair (Interactive)

Both Glen and Mai now appreciate that when things look the worst is when hope can break through.

"I could have just let Mai stay at her mom and dad's and let her believe it was all her fault. Then, for about one minute, I half-toyed with the idea that I'd show up at her parents' house like the hero on a white horse, riding in to save the day. But I got over that fast. I knew too much by that time, so I knew if I tried that it would be just another version of my rescuer song-and-dance routine."

Mai was silent for a moment. "When I saw Glen drive up at my parents', I didn't know what to think, what to say. But for some reason—I still don't know how this happened—I knew the running away was over. It had to be—both for him and our daughter."

Glen and Mai's newly forming willingness to tell the truth about their own part without blaming each other revolutionized everything about how they saw each other and their marriage.

"The 40-20-40 can work for anything—absolutely anything. It doesn't give anybody a place to hide, but it also lets you tell the truth without worrying about what happens next," Mai said.

"It takes practice though," Glen interjected, "figuring out what belongs to who, what caused who to get mad or hurt. And it's hard staying on your side of the street: each person has to figure out what's going on with no finger-pointing. But learning to do it changes everything. From our experience, the 40-20-40 proves that anything can be worked through, as long as you're both doing it."

Couples who practice the 40-20-40 can learn to see relationship issues as opportunities to build together rather than staking out territory to prove they're right. Mai and Glen discovered that even financial issues could be worked though using the 40-20-40.

"This was an area where we were both taking more blame than we should have for our money problems," Glen reflected. "We had a lot to learn about this, especially after the baby was born. Funny thing was our attitudes about money, which we'd never discussed with each other, ended up causing a lot more friction than the bad job we made of managing our money."

Empowerment

"Using the 40-20-40 to discuss finances wasn't something I even thought about before," Mai commented. "For the most part, I ignored my own money issues. I just spent, got more, and spent more. I didn't even let the words *financial insecurity* into my brain."

"And I'd never been close enough to anyone for it to even come up. My mother always just said, 'Money matters will be resolved—with money.' Only that didn't really work for us. The 40-20-40 got us looking straight at how we thought about money—especially the cocky way that I told myself that since I was the breadwinner, our money was my business. I even said so to Mai, and I wasn't very nice about it either."

"And I just took it," Mai said, "but it left me feeling as if nothing I did was worth anything because it couldn't be measured in dollars. But if I tried to suggest that taking care of the house and the baby had value, you'd come up with your 'after all I've done for you' line, which left me feeling as if I was next to nothing."

Empowerment is created when couples jointly develop strategies for communicating that teach both parties to feel that whatever happens in their relationship belongs to both of them rather than being a series of one-way transactions, randomly and powerlessly subject to each party's history, mood swings, or outside influences. The 40-20-40 is the venue for repair to whatever goes wrong, creates anxiety, or otherwise threatens mutual, unconditional caring.

"Just having these conversations without melting down still seems like a miracle," Mai said.

Empowerment is the stage in which the third entity, that is, the us-ness of the relationship itself, begins to reveal how it needs its own distinctive attention and care.

"Sex is another thing I've never been able to talk about with my partners," Glen said.

"Well—I'm Japanese. You never hear anybody talking about sex," Mai retorted.

When Glen and Mai started using the 40-20-40, they began to feel safe enough to tell one another how uneasy they felt about themselves as sex partners.

"I was the one who usually seemed to lose interest, except what I was really doing was managing my girlfriend's interest by withholding sex," Glen explained. "That way I could keep myself at a safe distance while at the same time forcing her to almost plead for it. It wasn't very nice. Not at all."

Mai countered, "I've always had a hard time believing I was sexually desirable. When Glen and I started doing the 40-20-40 around sex, it was scary. But before long, I could see how I was being the Audience when we were making love. It was the same thing I always did: I just accepted whatever you gave me and made sure I always told you how great it was. It never occurred to me that I had the right to even think about asking for what I wanted."

Compassionate empathy opens us up in unexpected, and even previously well-guarded, ways to who and what each other *really is*. This grows the willingness to give and receive, so the old habit of hiding becomes increasingly a violation of trust. Both partners become equally empowered to take equal ownership of that third entity, the relationship itself.

Alternatives

Using the 40-20-40 regularly keeps fresh how caretaking routines stand directly in the way of sharing and appreciating each other's resources. It undercuts the fear of making each person angry, and, thus, unable to examine each other's part in interpersonal problems. Once that barrier is pierced, the most mundane things—making monetary decisions, weekend plans, or spending time with children—become a way of building intimacy. Basically, as Mai observed, the 40-20-40 "enables me to ask for what I want or need without being afraid of making Glen angry."

Meeting his wife on an equal footing undercut Glen's feeling that he always had to protect and caretake her, freeing him to genuinely "respect, admire, and love her *exactly as she really is*." This let Mai off the hook for feeling she always had to show uncritical appreciation for whatever Glen did.

"I can let myself accept the care he offers, but I can also show him how to be a better partner by telling him what I need from him. That's a lot better than just getting more and more resentful because I'm afraid to let him know what I want."

Mutuality

Everything we've seen Mai and Glen accomplish is the result of learning to bring compassionate empathy to their interactions. The ultimate outcome is Mutuality, the M of the DREAM Sequence and the culmination of relationship sanity. The 40-20-40 is mutuality at its most practical and, as can be seen in Mai and Glen's story, unfolds as the principal tool of the entire DREAM Sequence.

"We've done hard work here," said Mai. "When you followed me to Japan, I was somehow able to surrender, but I had no idea what I was surrendering to. I never expected *this*—that what we were about to create was a situation in which you can care for someone and be cared for by him as partners without it turning into some kind of power trip for either of us.

"It still blows my mind," Mai continued, "that we found a way to look at the most insane things going on between us and use them to build real sanity into our marriage."

Compassionate empathy is the interior dynamic that makes it possible for people to jointly find their way into relationship sanity. Persevering along this path can be the solution to any issue, obstacle, or problem in a relationship, no matter how dark its recent or remote history.

Exercise: Revisiting Old Wounds *(Individuals)*

This exercise is a practicum for reclaiming old wounds and seeing beyond them to the possibility of no longer doing what you always did—a fundamental step toward relationship sanity.

Call to mind ways that you've protected yourself from vital, human experiences you felt that you wanted or needed but which frightened you, for example, friendship, companionship, love, passion, or even feeling vulnerable to someone you cared about.

Recall an experience of feeling alone or abandoned in which you later realized you had allowed an opportunity for caring human contact to slip away because you were afraid to let someone else know how vulnerable you felt. Perhaps you even disguised your feelings by using an irrelationship song-and-dance routine.

Focus on how your body reacts as you recall that experience of isolation—your breathing, heart rate, bodily tension, physical discomfort, or other physical effects of recalling painful experiences from the past.

Reimagine the scenario of missed opportunity, but this time, imagine that you accept your need for human contact and reveal it to another person. Imagine that she or he receives your candid disclosure of vulnerability with kindness. How does this reimagining change your experience of being in your body—the breathing, heartbeat, bodily discomforts, or tension?

As you examine this experience, imagine what might happen if other people in your life—family, neighbors, coworkers—were able to be truthful with themselves and others about this type of human need.

Staying on Target: Irrelationship versus Recovery

The DREAM Sequence is a technique for partners to see themselves through their partner's eyes—including the parts that are difficult, scary, and painful. Why is this important? Because, whether you're aware of them or not, these parts of yourself have a powerful effect on your lives, behaviors, and feelings—conscious or not. Not surprisingly, they have a huge impact on your relationships.

Key Takeaways

- The practice of expanded awareness strengthens our relationship with our emotions.
- Expanded awareness of our feelings improves our ability to reflect on questions such as the following.
    - o Do you fear rejection as you get close to others?
    - o Can you explore those feelings with curiosity and compassion for yourself?
    - o What gets in the way of doing so?
    - o How comfortable are you with looking at yourself in terms of assets and deficits?
- This kind of process is frustrating, difficult, and scary—and that's normal.

As you can see, compassionate empathy is not just a feeling or a thinking process: it involves *doing* and *living* in order to become more fully human. By embracing intimacy, empathy, vulnerability, and emotional investment, you will begin to realize the existence of the *third entity: you* and *me* are now *we*.

Now pause and look into each other's eyes. Then, using free association, discuss any thoughts or thought fragments, feelings, and reflections on where you were and where you're headed on the road of relationship sanity.

Chapter 10

Discovery

What is *discovered* in the Discovery stage of the DREAM Sequence is the absence of compassionate empathy. This is the primary obstacle to developing relationship sanity. Like the decision to break-up, separate, or divorce, Discovery is the one stage of the DREAM Sequence that may not include the participation, or even the awareness, of those with whom we're in irrelationship. So taking this step (which sometimes happens accidentally) is to come face-to-face with the threat of loss of your relationship, while simultaneously realizing it's a gamble you have to take if your relationship is to be rescued from the slow death of irrelationship.

Discovering how frightening intimacy actually feels is a process of beginning to experience the dissociated anxiety that our song-and-dance routines have kept out of our sight-lines. This is often preceded by an "emotional bottom," i.e., a state in which we can no longer suppress the pain created by the distance enforced by song-and-dance routines. Loneliness, resentment, and feeling ripped-off are common examples of this pain.

Irrelationship sabotages empathy, which is the primary channel of vulnerability and intimacy. Logically, the first step toward recovery is coming to terms with the scary idea that how we've been living isn't working anymore and that something has to change about how we relate to ourselves and everyone around us. This need for change is usually most noticeable when we realize how we've drifted from those most important to us—

especially our partners. On some subliminal level, we probably even realize that this is going to mean confronting the emotional pain that sidelined us into irrelationship in the first place.

Receiving a "D" Grade

"He's got six of the ten things I need from a husband," said Olivia of her husband Rodney, whom she'd recently separated from—again—and whom she was considering going back to—again.

"That's a 'D'," said Dr. B.

And though that's the first stage of the DREAM Sequence, Dr. B was attempting to show Olivia that after fifteen years of an on-again-off-again marriage to Rodney, she—not he—had given her husband a "D" grade: 6 out of 10—60%.

"He really, really needs me," Olivia pleaded.

Rodney, like Olivia's mother, was chronically depressed. For Olivia, it was like bees to honey: it didn't matter that she was not physically attracted to Rodney; that he'd never held a regular job; or that their sex life had mostly been confined to the three times they'd decided to have a child.

"And now," continued Olivia, "there isn't much else—except that he needs me."

"So is that a good thing or a bad thing?" asked Dr. B.

Everything about Olivia seemed geared to the job of being Rodney's caretaker: he was a seemingly passive but deeply depressed person who, at the same time, required that no matter what Olivia wanted and needed for herself, her desires had to come second: she had to be willing to put them aside to accommodate whatever care needs he had, whenever he had them. The deeper pact was, however, that their hand-in-glove song-and-dance routines would bury both of their hopes and dreams, creating a powerful ambivalence that paralyzed them within a terror that held them in place—at least, (for Olivia) episodically. Irrelationship was the acting out—enactment—that protected Olivia and Rodney from knowing even their own hearts' desires. However, though they'd seemingly obliterated their awareness of their hopes and dreams, needs and desires, the influence of these dreams and desires raged on beneath the surface while irrelationship kept them protected from their deep desire to make and share love with another.

Olivia continued, "So I woke up to find myself almost forty years old, and feeling as if I were the only adult in my family. Oh, and that includes Liam."

During one of Rodney and Olivia's numerous separations, Liam came on the scene, throwing a wrench in the gears of an otherwise effectively functioning irrelationship situation. For Olivia, Liam was a kind of consolation prize—was "just about everything that Rodney isn't—especially sexually." Liam had a successful real-estate business and was twenty years older than Olivia. He had two grown children and was married to a woman he claimed he didn't love, though they still occasionally had sex, sort of as "a duty thing," he said.

"But—wow!" exclaimed Olivia. "With Liam it was like nothing I'd ever experienced in my life. 'So why,' I began to ask myself, 'why can't we go riding off into the sunset? Or is Liam caretaking his wife like I do Rodney—a wife he says is old and unwell? And into the bargain, is he making sure his kids aren't further casualties of the bad marriage he and his wife can't get themselves out of? That's a big part of the discussion I've had with myself about Liam over and over again—kind of an extension of how I've needed to see myself.

"Only Liam was very jealous: he was constantly worried that something might happen, that I might actually have sex with Rodney again; but he was even more worried that I'd find a younger, available man whom I'd be able to use as a way to really get out of my marriage and just walk away from these once-in-awhile escapes with him. And he knew I wasn't a hundred-percent satisfied because I was the one who would sometimes complain that I wanted more. But even though he didn't really give an inch in that way, he couldn't stand the idea of me being with someone else—even my own husband!

"During one of my separations from Rodney, when Liam and I could have been together anytime we wanted, Liam demanded that I take a lie-detector test so he could be sure I hadn't been with anyone else!

"Obviously, it was a frying-pan-into-the-fire scenario. I jumped from Rodney to Liam, using Liam as a kind of compensation. I told myself over and over that great sex was exactly the compensation I deserved for how miserable I'd been with Rodney. But, it turned out that taking care of Liam's ego was the back-end price I had to pay for hot sex. Only things started to go kind of crazy in ways I wasn't expecting and didn't really like. I think the first sign was that it was getting harder and harder for him to get off during sex. Then he seemed to become less and less concerned about whether I was actually 'there' or not, as long as I took his phone calls and showed up when I was 'supposed to.' In other words, he still expected me to be his caretaker, same as Rodney did. As far as Liam was concerned, that's what it all came down to: it was my job to make sure he got what he wanted *when* he wanted it. And I was expected to let him know that I *loved* being in that role, as if it were some kind of privilege. During sex he even wanted me to call him 'Big Daddy,' as in, 'Choke me, Big Daddy.' But it was all just another way he demanded that I take care of him, as if I was some kind of drug that made him feel alive, gave him some kind of relief from how 'horribly depressing' his home life was. The fact that I was required to *act as if* what Liam gave me was *good enough*—when it wasn't—filled me with a familiar dread.

"Well, for a good while, I accepted how he treated me. I mean, it *was* thrilling at first—I thought doing that hardcore taboo stuff meant that something *real* was going on between us. But as he got more and more demanding without really giving anything in return, I started to see that the reverse side of the Liam coin looked strangely like my life with Rodney. Although, I can't deny that for a while there, I did feel that Liam was giving me some of those ten things I've always told myself I needed. But, overall, truthfully, it was an 'F'."

A "D" or an "F"—what kind of choice is that? It's an irrelationship type of choice, and both are great places to hide from intimacy. In a sense, Olivia's choices were working so well at keeping her blockaded against real intimacy that it was extremely difficult for her to realize—to Discover—how irrelationship was "protecting" her and to accept the remedy for it.

"I'd crash through bottom after bottom—come to a point with one of them then I'd bounce over to the other. I just couldn't see, couldn't understand, what had happened to me that made me put up with that Big Daddy craziness. But at the same time, what kept bringing me back to Rodney? Why would I even think that's an option—*now*? Only, it's still true that I have trouble imagining Rodney fending for himself—that if he didn't have me to look after him, he would somehow go off the deep end.

"But you know what's funny?" Olivia continued, "My dad died of a heart attack when I was ten; and my mom basically spent the rest of my childhood in bed, depressed and taking pain killers. It was hard to believe it happened to him. My father was tall, dark, handsome, strong—well, I thought he was strong—like Liam! And I secretly dreaded that if I fell in love and had a family, that guy, whoever he was, would disappear somehow, maybe even die like my dad did, and leave me in a lurch like what happened to my mom. In fact, when Rodney started getting sick and depressed, it felt like everything I was afraid was going to happen was actually happening! Rodney did all the same things my dad did: he smoked, drank a lot, and ate like he *wanted* to have a heart attack. And I knew that if I didn't save him from himself, it was going to happen to him the same way. So my job became to make sure that *wasn't* what happened. I made sure he ate right, cut down on his drinking, went to the gym; jeez, it was ridiculous: I even got him a hypnotist to help him quit smoking. I sort of thought I was on a wild spin on the cliché of marrying my father—only what I'd actually done was married my mom! My mom, who disappeared in her bed and her pills after my father died, also demanded this twisted kind of caretaking. So it was totally out of the blue when I realized that my bouncing back and forth between Liam and Rodney was just a version of me when I was a kid, doing my best to take care of them so that they could take care of me—exactly like I did for my mom. When Dad died, she acted as if it was something he *did to her*, making her the martyr-victim. And there I was—this kid who needed somebody to look after me. But the only way I could get her to focus on me at all was to pretend that she was a great mom—that, even though she was so 'sick,' I was *so appreciative of everything she did* for me, things were so 'hard' for her!"

It was on a day that Olivia was talking about the lie-detector test that the "married my mother" realization began to dawn, and a dim light began to flicker on. She started questioning at that time whether her life was worth a "D-level" relationship, but it would still be some time before she would make her final escape from both the "D" and the "F" versions of irrelationship. But she kept working at it until she started seeing the part her own choices played in her repetitive cycle of disappointment and pain. That was her window of opportunity to begin to believe she could make other choices besides a depressed Rodney or an abusive but electrifying Liam. Discovering she didn't have to do what she had always done was her first step on the road of relationship sanity.

"I believed I was doomed to a life of caretaking either for Liam or for Rodney—a life that, one way or another, felt safe because it felt so much like those years caretaking I did for my mother after Dad died. It was so weird to realize that I was an Audience who willingly contorted my needs and desires to make them feel that I got what I really needed from them, which, like my mom, neither of them *could* give. Rodney's incompetence was reminiscent of my mom's and gave me a way to be doting and dutiful. Liam's moods and martyrdom, on the other hand, were like my mother's dramatic emotional extremes, including her self-pity. Somehow, he knew how to use his victimhood and jealousy to manipulate me into not leaving him."

"So, now," Dr B said, "you're done with Liam, but still convinced that Rodney needs you? Still six out of ten?"

Olivia paused. Then replied, "A 'D'? Do you think there's no other way to spin that?"

This time, however, the "D" was for "Discovery".[1]

"Yeah," Olivia said, answering her own question, "It's still a 'D,' but what a different 'D'! This is a *real* new beginning!"

Exercise: Discovery *(Couples)*

The goal of this exercise is to identify overt or covert behaviors that are part of caretaking routines intended to keep your distance from your partner. The following table provides examples.

Caretaking Behavior/Routine	Example of How It Plays Out in Your Relationship	Impact This Behavior Has on Your Relationship
Unilateral financial management	I manage all of our finances and make everyone else feel guilty for spending without my approval.	Keeping the burden of financial management to myself makes me feel resentful toward my partner, while my partner feels excluded, untrusted, and infantilized.
Tolerance for unacceptable behavior	I pretend I'm okay with how I'm treated but come up with excuses for not having sex.	My denied feelings undercut my attraction to my partner, which creates coolness in other parts of our relationship.

After reviewing the two general behavior examples in the table, scan the types of interactions you have with your partner to identify particular caretaking routines you share.

- Look for specific behaviors and verbal exchanges that are characteristic of your shared routine of giving and receiving caretaking.
- Describe ways that your caretaking routines serve as protection against empathy, intimacy, vulnerability, and emotional investment.
- Discuss how using these routines affects your connection with one another. Refer back to the GRAFTS table in Chapter 2 as needed.

Defects

Asset Mapping (see the asset-mapping exercises for individuals and for couples in Chapter 5) opens the door to the 40-20-40 by helping us to see how we contribute to what happens in our relationships. Some aspects of this may be thought of as defects. Shared openness and honesty about them creates a safe space in which partners can discover and step away from isolating habits that keep them from offering and accepting support. As Glen and Mai saw, this vital skill turns problems into opportunities for building intimacy.

Exercise: Avoidance (Couples)

The following exercise explores how avoiding relationship challenges affects your feelings.

- Recall an incident in any relationship—even in the distant past—in which you deliberately chose not to confront an issue or relationship problem because you were afraid of the feelings that would result from it.
- Mentally examine the incident: What was going through your head? What did you choose to do? What feelings were you left with afterward?
- Can you remember other occasions in which you made similar choices for similar reasons? What happened in those cases?

This type of self-critique isn't intended to imply that avoiding certain situations or relationships is a mistake. The goal is to understand your own processes better and improve your decision-making about the desirability of a relationship.

After sharing your responses to the bulleted items, create a two-column table to assess your interactions with one another. On the left side, write down your avoidance patterns, and on the right, write down how you think your partner reacted to your avoidance. Label the columns "Avoidance Action" and "Partner's Reaction," respectively.

Now let's go further. Create another table. On the left side of the table, list avoidance behaviors that you have begun to discover may be aspects of irrelationship. On the right, list behaviors of your partner that may indicate that she or he colluded with your avoidance behavior. Label the columns "Irrelationship Avoidance Action (Yourself, Your Partner)" and "Partner's Reaction (Collusion and Collaboration)," respectively.

Keep your two-column table handy: as you continue through the book and its exercises, it will be useful as a quick reference when analyzing feelings and behaviors.

The Platform for Change

"Acceptance is the platform for change." One of the authors lays down this cardinal principle to couples that come to him for therapy. David and John often needed to remind themselves and one another of this maxim—especially during high-pressure moments that came long after they adopted twin girls.

"Your whole thing about acceptance didn't make much sense to me at first," David said. "But we just kept getting into emotional jams that we couldn't work through. So we kept using the same workaround: We walked away from it. We ignored it. And little by little, life at home started getting darker and darker. In fact, it got so bad that we avoided being at home at the same time.

"Then one day in session, I got it. It was like you'd turned on this light in a dark room, and I finally opened my eyes: either I accept John exactly as he is or I let him go. The only alternative was for things to just keep getting darker, and God knows neither of us wanted the girls to grow up in *that*."

"Yep," John kicked in. "Before I met David, I was in a relationship that became a cold war. And it made me feel so insecure that I built this fortress inside me, and I wasn't letting anybody in ever again no matter how attracted I was to him. At the same time, I knew I was crazy about David, but deep down all I could hear was 'Intruder Alert!' Well, I did my damnedest to shut it all down by shutting *me* down and keeping him out. But my defenses missed a beat, and I was fool enough to give him my number when he asked if he could text me. And he *did* text, and I *did* get an instant buzz, which I shut down with a resentment chaser. Who did he think he was, intruding on me like that when I barely knew him? You think I told myself I thought I liked him in those moments? Hell, NO, I didn't go there!"

Despite the lessons of the past, David and John fell uncontrollably in love, even while admitting to each other that they weren't sure they were prepared for where it might take them—especially after they'd confided in each other their desire for children.

In their fourth year together, they began the adoption process, which was complicated, expensive, and stressful. But keeping their eyes on the prize helped them to avoid thinking about buried trust issues that quietly hounded both of them. When the girls were born, both David and John told themselves that they didn't have to worry about losing each other anymore because that was no longer an option: they owned each other. But that still didn't eliminate the unease or build trust and companionship; and it certainly didn't provide any clues about how to build those things into their marriage.

"I still felt in love, but everything I tried to do at home to help with the girls seemed clumsy and often backfired, which just made John mad. Sometimes I even felt like he was lying in wait for me to mess up. Then when I did—which I *always* did—I'd get so angry that I felt as if I hated him. And he *knew* it, but it was like he didn't get it, like it was *my* problem—mine to fix." David brushed away tears. "It was like he was waiting for me to come to my own conclusion that they'd all be better off without me."

Irrelationship prevents mutual acceptance in two ways:

1. A couple unconsciously agrees to maintain emotional distance in order to not feel vulnerable to each other.
2. Both partners deliberately lay down conditions that must be met in order to allow closeness but adopt unconscious attitudes and mechanisms that ensure that the conditions won't be met.

"The most important lesson I've learned in therapy is how useless finger-pointing is. In AA they call it 'taking someone else's inventory.' It doesn't help anything, but I became an expert," David said. "In fact, my criticizing John was so effective that he got to where he knew in advance when it was coming. I could see his eyes glaze over before I even opened my mouth. It didn't matter what I was getting on him about—whether it was about me, about the house, the girls, he could tell it was coming. And when I got started, the room would actually feel like it was getting dark. It felt good to dump on him like that at first, but before very long, I'd started to feel worse after I let him have it more often than I did before."

John added, "Meanwhile, I'd be riding my high horse about how much I did for the family, compared to him, the stay-at-home dad. God, it was ugly. The very things I'd told him I loved about him I was now criticizing. It was total betrayal, but it was convenient because it kept me from looking at *me*.

"When we went into therapy I had no idea why this was happening. It finally came out, though, that the way I saw my responsibility for David *and* those two girls made me feel almost useless around the house. So I got to where I stayed away, out of the house, as much as I could—which just made him madder and madder at me. And no damn wonder. But there we were: two intelligent men at such cross purposes that we couldn't figure out a way to even talk about how frustrated we were."

After a pause, John continued, "We'd made it impossible for either of us to appreciate, or even accept, what the other brought to the table. It was a safe, noncommittal way to be in a relationship without actually being invested in each other."

"The irony of it all," David said, "was that, for once, with John, I hadn't chosen 'the wrong kind of guy.' But that didn't make me, or either of us actually, any less scared of where we were headed. So I hid behind being an at-home dad, and he hid out as breadwinner."

"I loved David," John added. "And it was scary—not because I felt there was anything big wrong with him, but because I *didn't* think so. So what did I do? I started telling myself all these bullshit stories about how he didn't appreciate me anymore and all that mattered to him now was the girls. It was such a crock."

John and David's mutual appreciation and acceptance seemed to be a true case of love at first sight, but that didn't erase their histories. The impasse they reached in their inability to cope with success and communicate through distress brought them into therapy. That choice was the opening of the door to discovering how invested in irrelationship they were.

Exercise: Discovery and Compassionate Empathy *(Couples)*

Exploring the experience of Discovery improves the understanding of what irrelationship is, why we use it, and how it works.

The following questions can help you to see specific instances of how you and your partner use irrelationship techniques to keep your distance from each other.

- What irrelationship behaviors, such as caretaking, fixing, or rescuing, have I used on my partner? What's going on in my life or our lives when I do it? Is my partner aware of it? How does she or he respond?
- What kinds of behaviors have I expected my partners to use as a kind of solution to my problems, so I feel less anxious? Have the exercises up to this point in this book changed how I see that expectation?
- What is the difference between loving someone and caretaking them?
- How has my perception of love and caretaking been changed by using this book?

When you're finished, compare your responses to your responses to the Caretaking Agreements Exercise in Chapter 2 and discuss the similarities and differences, as well as how your perspectives may have evolved.

Exercise: Blocking Reciprocity *(Individuals)*

The isolation created by irrelationship is partly caused by not allowing free give-and-take between partners—usually because one partner needs to believe she or he is the hero, problem-solver-fixer in the relationship, while the other partner is her or his fix-it project. The unanticipated effect of demeaning the other partner in that way leaves both people feeling strangely disconnected and, over time, increasingly resentful.

The healthy alternative is reciprocity—a means of exchange in which each person values and accepts with genuine appreciation what the other has to offer. The following exercise explores ways of thinking and behaving that block reciprocity.

- Write down words and phrases you use when you're blaming yourself for something that didn't go as you'd hoped, planned, or expected.
- Write down what you're feeling in the moments you bash yourself with those words.
- How do those words or phrases connect with the idea of self-protection explored in this book?

Learning to explore how you use negative ideas about yourself for self-protection is a vital piece of Discovery.

Exercise: Joint Compassion—Unblocking Reciprocity (Couples)

The next chapter explores the process of repairing damaged relationships by exposing the very vulnerabilities that we've spent our lives hiding from ourselves and others. But before proceeding, let's reprise and riff on the Joint Compassion Meditation Exercise introduced in Chapter 1. This will be practically indispensable to continuing with the DREAM Sequence because it promotes better understanding of ourselves and, therefore, enables us to make better choices in how we navigate relationships.

You may do this practice together or at different times or in separate places but avoid doing it at a point in your schedule in which you're liable to fall asleep.

- Set a time limit of three to five minutes.
- Sit quietly in a comfortable, seated position with your feet flat on the floor, your head slightly tilted down, and your eyes partially open, looking at a spot a few feet in front of you. Focus on your breathing.
- Take note of the thoughts passing through your mind. Then return your attention to your breath.

- If you become disturbed because of the variety of thoughts going through your head, remind yourself that this practice isn't for identifying anything good/bad or right/wrong about you or anybody else: its purpose is to practice nonjudgmentally observing what passes through your mind as the DREAM Sequence unfolds for you.
- After the allotted time ends, write down any thoughts and feelings that came up during the exercise. Considering each item separately, see if you're able to connect it with particular ideas that you've gotten from using this book.
- Share with your partner what you've seen and discovered. If you're not comfortable doing that, or not in every case, tell your partner: the act of disclosing discomfort is, itself, empowering and promotes intimacy.

Staying on Target: Irrelationship and Isolation versus Discovery and Connection

Both (or all) parties involved in an irrelationship don't necessarily reach Discovery at the same time. As mentioned earlier, it usually begins with a breakthrough of the anxiety and other negative feelings against which irrelationship is becoming increasingly ineffective. As a threat to how you've long been coping, Discovery can be terrifying.

Key Takeaways

- We have an understanding and acceptance of hitting bottom—a way of realizing that you're trapped in the song-and-dance routine of irrelationship.
- Hitting bottom is paradoxically revealed to us when feelings of anxiety and isolation break through the irrelationship defense system.
- We are beginning to have a better sense of what irrelationship is at this stage and we are becoming willing to change.

- We developed tools for being increasingly able to see how our song-and-dance routine has been a failure and have begun to want to change how we have been living.

Now that you have an understanding of yourself, yourselves, your sense of Self-Other (especially in an expanding sense of multiple self-experience), your song-and-dance routines, and your irrelationship patterns, answer the following questions related to each other or anyone else who threatens to become important in your life (e.g., a partner, a spouse, a parent, an adult child).

- Do I keep trying to fix or rescue the person I have been working with throughout these exercises (and/or that other person who keeps coming to mind)?
- Do I keep hoping that person will fix or rescue me?
- Do I equate "loving" with "taking care of"?
- What has that looked and felt like with my partner throughout this process?
- What does that look and feel like when I imagine it applied to the other people—and the person I am focusing on—in my life?
- Do I keep "doing for" my partner, even when I receive little in return?
- Does my partner keep "doing for" me?

Now pause and look at each other. Use free association to discuss any thoughts or thought fragments, feelings, reflections, and analysis of where you were and where you're headed—individually and as a couple—along the road of recovery from irrelationship, the road of relationship sanity.

Chapter 11

Repair

Just as the isolation created by irrelationship leads to damaged relationships, the repair process must be interactive if healthy interdependence[1] is to displace isolation. This reverses the adaptation undertaken by individuals who, in early childhood, were left alone with the anxiety they suffered as a result of inadequate caregiving—anxiety that never resolved later in life.[2]

No issue, problem or blow-up is too large or too small to be addressed effectively by the interactive repair process, i.e., the 40-20-40—the technique that teaches us to build reciprocity and mutuality. This includes any type of issue, from a bad experience in a restaurant to extramarital affairs to violence. In fact, processing such experiences through the 40-20-40 adds trust to the relationship that would be difficult to create without sharing the process of failure and repair. In short, such experiences build relationship sanity.

Exercise: History of Repair *(Individuals)*

In the following table, there are examples of changes one partner made to address a relationship issue without consulting her or his partner. Reading left to right, the table lists what the net effect was.

Measures You've Taken to Address Relationship Issues or Conflicts	What This Measure Looks Like	The Measure's Impact on Your Relationship
I work double shifts, in order to be able to pay all the household bills.	I take full responsibility for all our finances, which allows me to congratulate myself on how much I contribute to our relationship.	My self-congratulating deteriorates into seeing myself as a martyr, complete with self-pity, feelings of exploitation, resentment and bitterness.
I do all the childcare twenty-four/seven to save my breadwinner husband from additional stress.	I manage all the kids' activities, which keeps them out of the house even when their father is around.	I feel resentful that all kids' nonmaterial needs fall on me. Meanwhile, they have little emotional connection with their father even though we all live together.

Now write down examples of specific measures you've taken to address relationship issues or conflicts without consulting your partner and describe the outcome.

Exercise: History of Repair *(Couples)*

The next table gives examples of identified relationship issues that are addressed with joint problem-solving, which instills joint accountability and increases trust and intimacy.

Measures or Strategies Taken Jointly to Address Relationship Issues	What This Measure Looks Like	Impact This Measure Has on Your Relationship
We're deliberately accountable to each other for our financial contributions to the household.	Transparency and accountability improves the quality of our financial decision-making.	Practicing financial accountability has created increased mutual trust in other aspects of our relationship.
When processing a relationship issue, instead of finger-pointing, we take turns disclosing to each other how we feel we contribute to our issues.	When a problem arises, we try to practice addressing it in this way as soon as possible after we identify it.	We feel safe with each other when we have to discuss an issue.

Using the table as a guide, list ways that you've tried to fix relationship issues together, what the outcome was, and why you think it did or didn't work. It might be useful to experiment with the 40-20-40 and try to gain insight into your experience, thus far, of your caretaking roles and trying to "fix" your relationship.

Honeymoon to Hell and Back Again

"What a great year we've had," Evelyn reflected. "The honeymoon didn't even go away even after Eli was born."

Jacob, Evelyn's second husband, agreed, "I still hate leaving the house in the morning!"

From her first marriage, Evelyn had learned an important lesson the hard way: believing nothing's wrong doesn't mean nothing's wrong.

Her marriage to Jacob, however, was a totally different scenario. After nearly two years of what seemed like marital perfection, Jacob and Evelyn woke one morning—literally it happened almost overnight—to find that something had changed in their feelings for one another. They had no idea how this could be and certainly didn't connect it with other life-events that had created a sudden major change in their household: Evelyn had lost her job. Of course, this was a knock to her ego, one that Evelyn wasn't able to bring herself to talk about with Jacob. It was also a blow to their financial plans centering on their new baby. However, most destructive of all, perhaps, was that Evelyn and Jacob were afraid of creating further emotional upset by confiding in each other how worried they were about their new financial uncertainty.

Up to this point, they'd believed themselves to be a good team and used their sexual connection to weather relationship difficulties. Suddenly, however, that solution didn't work. Finally they hesitatingly agreed they were going to have to sell their apartment—a predictably disturbing and disheartening decision because of the passion they'd shared and nurtured in that space, though they admitted it wasn't a suitable home for a new young family.

Both Evelyn and Jacob had histories under their belts that were a set-up for irrelationship. Her previous marriage had been built—and failed—around her insistence on her role as a Performer. Post-mortem therapy, however, convinced her that awareness of irrelationship would prevent her re-enacting that role in future relationships. It didn't work out that way: Jacob's having grown up in a family in which he played Audience to his narcissistic father was right on time when they encountered their marital-financial crisis. He was only too willing to stifle his own anxiety in the crisis and affirm Evelyn as star of the show even after she became unemployed. The end result was that they blocked one another's need to share the crisis and their feelings, especially the anxiety it created in both of them.

"Ignoring our own and each other's emotions quickly made us feel that our connection had just vanished. I told myself that stress from having a baby and the financial thing exposed the truth: we just weren't suited for each other—it had all been a big mistake. We ended up threatening each other with divorce without ever having talked about what had happened since I lost my job."

"Well," Jacob rejoined, "what really did the damage was how abandoned we both felt—abandoned by each other! And no wonder: nobody was talking and nobody was listening. It didn't take long for it to turn into a game of one-upmanship and mutually assured destruction, complete with talk about divorce and throwing our wedding rings at each other."

"Yeah," Evelyn filled in. "I got so sick of how you obnoxiously held your hand up to make sure I saw you taking off your wedding ring—until finally I'd had enough of it and flushed both of them. God, how I was screaming inside! Only now I know I was screaming *for* you as much as *at* you!"

Reaching the Bottom and Choosing Repair

Interactive repair is often a hard sell. Jacob and Evelyn were both at a place where the choice of finding a way to start over was only slightly more appealing than conceding failure and walking away. They believed that having had a new son was what swayed them toward not compounding the disaster.

"At first it was all but impossible to believe that our bitterness was exactly where Jacob and I had to go to find the answer," Evelyn commented.

When Jacob and Evelyn first tried using the 40-20-40, or Self-Other Assessment, keeping their focus on their own contribution to any issue totally went against the grain. But staying with 40-20-40 paid off: it finally started to create a calm enough space for them to remember how much they actually loved each other and find a new footing—or, perhaps, rediscover the old footing—for their being together.

This is the model for interactive repair: it allows partners to negotiate in the 20-percent shared space in the middle while owning the feelings, missteps, and defenses that each contributed to the outbreak of crisis—their respective 40 percent. Perhaps the most surprising benefit of this process is that, through it, participants allow themselves to be seen, known, and accepted as they *really are*, which is precisely what irrelationship is designed to prevent.

Reminiscing about past relationships, Evelyn said, "I could see a long line of people—and not just boyfriends—that I kind of forced into caring about me because I made them feel better. And it hasn't been easy to let go of; in fact, I don't think I even knew it was happening. But it's how I controlled pretty much all my relationships with others. And then I lost my job, and poor Jacob was stuck with somebody who was not only totally lost, but I had no idea what to do with myself or how to *really* fix anything."

"And for once," Jacob said, "all I was looking for, really, was my wife. I didn't give a damn about any of the other stuff. Screw the job: I needed *her*. The 'everything's okay' stuff didn't help me or anything else. I just needed Evelyn to show up, to be there."

"But," Evelyn remembered, "the only thing we seemed to be able to stick to was fighting. It was lousy all the time—even when we weren't arguing. But I guess—no, I know—at least the fighting kept us connected.

"Well, then this couple we know got us interested in a couples' group that practiced what was basically the 40-20-40: listening without blaming, no matter how angry you felt. Sometimes it was hard to go to that group.

And sometimes it was hard to stay for the whole thing. In fact, sometimes I didn't. But we went, and we kept going. And we heard and saw other couples going through what we went through—or worse. Some of it was horrible—threats, violence, screwing around, you name it. And there they were, right there in that group, putting it back together, basically, by just telling the truth about how they *felt* when all that stuff was going on. One guy even talked about how he was feeling when he got violent with his boyfriend. I don't understand why, but when you get honest like that, it somehow starts changing the chemistry of the whole thing."

"Yeah," Jacob added. "For some reason that I still don't get, when you expose yourself like that—or when your wife does—it's like you're going back to what made you fall in love in the first place. And when *that* starts coming back, you almost don't have any choice but to listen. Then, before you know what's happening, you begin to trust and depend on each other like you never did before."

By talking with one another about their vulnerability, Evelyn and Jacob began repairing what had been wrong from the very beginning of their relationship as well as what had been wrong in themselves individually even before they met. The bonus is that sharing this process created intimacy they'd never enjoyed with anyone, ever.

"I doubt if I would ever have been able to figure this out," said Jacob. "That word *Audience* is exactly where I was: I was a good Audience so my partner would feel good. I had no clue that doing that actually created a barrier, so we could keep real issues out of our sightline. The two of us doing this—Evelyn performing and me watching—meant we never had to talk about anything that made us nervous or we were worried about. We had our deepest, scariest feelings on the shelf—or more like a locked cabinet! Funny thing is that the first place it all began to fall apart was in the bedroom, where it had been so good before. But too many things can't be faked when you're naked together. Well, when the sex started to go south, it added big time to how mad we were at each other. It was like betrayal but without any infidelity."

"Learning how to do this doesn't mean we never fight anymore," Evelyn laughed. "But our anger doesn't last as long—usually. And we both know when something isn't right, we can ask for a 40-20-40 and get to the bottom of it before we start going off the rails without knowing why. And each time we do it, everything about being together gets a little better—including the sex!"

"But it sure was embarrassing," Jacob said, "when we had to go back to the jeweler: those rings had been custom made for us and how do you explain that we'd lost not one but *both of them?*"

Exercise: Chronic Issues *(Couples)*

Identify one or two ongoing issues in your relationship that you're willing to work on together using the techniques in this book, including the DREAM Sequence technique that you're reading about now.

Individually, write brief descriptions of the two issues. Then under each item, write your part in that issue. If either partner doesn't want to write about her or his part, or is unsure what her or his part is, then make a note of that.

Next share what you've written with your partner. If areas of disagreement about the issues arise, write those down too.

From the list, agree on one item to work on together. It's best not to use an issue on which you're at an uncomfortable stalemate or which is creating resentment. Instead, choose something you can talk about honestly without creating bad feelings between you.

Having reached agreement, discuss together the following questions.

1. What do you think this issue is *really* about? For example, if the issue has to do with dividing up household tasks, do you believe one party is avoiding a particular task for a reason other than that she or he simply doesn't like doing it? Are underlying or undiscussed feelings or attitudes involved? Do you think your partner should give you a pass because of something else you do?

2. Why is this a problem that you both believe needs to be addressed rather than allowing it to "ride"?

3. What impact, direct and indirect, has this issue had on other aspects of your relationship? On your family, your household, and beyond?

4. What benefit do you get from not resolving this issue?

5. How could you begin to resolve the issue by breaking it up into smaller or more manageable parts?

6. How does open discussion change your perception of the issue and your willingness to work on it?

Exercise: How Am I *Not* Interactive? *(Couples)*

To make interactive repair work, all parties have to feel safe. That's a big reason for the rule against finger-pointing when doing the 40-20-40. But committing to repair also has to include committing to honesty about your own part in what goes wrong between you and your partner.

Both parties have to be willing to honestly try to answer this question: How does my part in relationship issues prevent our finding solutions?

For this exercise, you and your partner write out her or his own personal traits or behaviors that may get in the way of joint problem solving. Remember, according to the rules of the 40-20-40, your part cannot account for more than 60 percent and no less than 40 percent of what happens between you. With practice, the middle 20 percent—the space for negotiation—grows as you become less attached to what you think you believe about yourself or your partner, which makes you more able to rethink how you understand any given conflict—a major marker of relationship sanity.

Exercise: Attempts at Problem-Solving *(Couples)*

The best way to get around taking your partner's inventory, or finger-pointing, is to take your own. In fact, it's the only way the 40-20-40 works. Otherwise you just add to the mess that has to be cleaned up for the relationship to become healthy.

Jointly think of problems in your life together—either interpersonal or household issues—that you have both identified and tried unsuccessfully to solve. Then write down how each of you perceives that issue, how you've tried to fix it, and what you think has stood in the way of fixing it.

Going off the rails in crises or even in less serious conflicts and then putting it back together sums up interactive repair. But it requires the ability to share the process through hearing and understanding the experience of your partner with that issue—in other words, through compassionate empathy. Learning to use that process routinely takes users through the rest of the DREAM Sequence.

Exercise: Compassionate Interactive Repair *(Couples)*

Take another opportunity to practice the Joint Compassion Meditation Exercise from Chapter 1. It's been tweaked here to highlight its purpose in approaching the work of interactive repair. Remember that nonjudgmental observation of your thoughts *and* what your partner shares is vital to moving forward productively.

- Set a timer for three to five minutes. In a comfortable, seated position, sit quietly together with your attention on your own breath.
- Note the stream of thoughts passing through your mind and then return your attention to your breath.
- As often as necessary, remind yourself that this practice has no right/wrong or good/bad: its purpose is to learn about your thoughts, your impulses, and the things that you are uneasy about or even resist.
- After the allotted time, make notes about how the idea of interactive repair affects you, both positively and negatively.
- Share with one another about how what you're experiencing, jointly and in your own thoughts, may affect your relationship.

Staying on Target: Indignation and Self-Righteousness versus Repair

Compassionate empathy opens the door to intimacy, making repair *interactive*. This interactivity creates the space for relationship sanity. This is where the rubber hits the road as you're challenged to develop healthy interdependency (versus dependency) so you can recover from irrelationship.

Key Takeaways

- We recognize how irrelationship affects you as an individual as well as how it affects us as a couple.
- We learned how to overcome natural resistance and repression and are coming to understand and break out of dissociation.
- We learned how to engage our partner in an interactive repair process.
- We understand how our habit of hiding from connection with others can be changed.
- We have come to believe that we can safely accept what others have to offer—especially those closest to us.
- We learned that listening, caring, and being present for and with each other can become new ways of managing anxiety.
- We let go of the idea that somebody has to be blamed.
- We recognized the patterns of interaction between our partners and ourselves.
- We recognized and communicated about themes of conflict.
- We recognized ways that our song-and-dance routines impact conflict—its eruption, handling, and resolution—in other relationships.
- We developed a roadmap for using our experience of conflict resolution—with each other and others—to more fully and consciously engage in interactive repair.

- We understand how the concept and practice of interactive repair—using each conflict as an opportunity for building empathy, intimacy, and mutual trust and reliance—is changing our relationship.
- We addressed what impact interactive repair can have on other relationships in our lives.

Going off the rails in conflict or crisis and then getting back on the rails together is what happens in interactive repair. The shared commitment to working together to fix what's wrong resolves conflict and creates a shared space of intimacy, as well as a growing sense of mutual trust and reliance. Along the way it generates profound, durable buy-in into the repair process, which improves the quality of decision-making for the couple, both as individuals and jointly. This increases trust and interpersonal reliance, which further resolves barriers to intimacy.

Each shared act of Repair is, by definition, reciprocal and complementary. This includes repairing everything from minor misunderstandings to devastating crises, including infidelity and violence. Not only can the 40-20-40 address each incident of "getting it wrong," but it can convert such experiences into new dimensions of trust that would be less likely to develop without such episodes.

Once again, pause, look at each other, and then use free association to discuss thoughts or thought fragments, feelings, reflections, and analysis of where you were and where you now see yourselves along the road of relationship sanity.

Chapter 12

Empowerment

Relationships are empowering to the extent that their participants are able to solve relationship issues and problems jointly. Mutual empowerment solidifies a healthy, realistic commitment to continuing the work started in Discovery and Repair.[1] A child's capacity to be alone depends on her or his ability to take in and internalize a sense of the mother's compassionate, comforting, and loving presence even when absent from her.[2] This matures into the capacity to regulate anxiety, self-soothe, and experience authenticity—abilities fundamental to the capacity for intimacy. The paradox of empowerment is that it allows us to build alliances and functional healthy interdependencies that enhance our capacity to manage *our own* lives.[3]

Functional Synergies: Top Dog, Underdog, Equal Dog

After making it over several early-stage developmental hurdles, one of the partners of a start-up asked his two colleagues, "Is working together so closely bringing up sibling issues for you two?"

"I wouldn't call it sibling issues," Ian responded. "It's more like being married."

Danny agreed.

Ian was highly invested in the creative elements of their project, while Danny focused on the business-related elements of their young company.

Their third partner, Greg, whose interest lay in product refinement and developing internet-based marketing, kept himself in the background. Though Ian and Danny had different opinions about which aspects of the business were vital to its survival, each was able during business meetings to validate his colleagues' work. Whenever friction developed between Ian and Danny, Greg would try to remain silent, but, when pressed, he would attempt to placate both partners.

From the beginning, they'd agreed to treat one another as equals in all aspects of their business. Nevertheless, top dog/underdog dynamics surfaced at times between Ian and Danny during their first year. The upshot of all of this was that the protestations of equality were, at best, naïve, wishful thinking that allowed the partners to avoid the emotional risks connected with working closely in a shared project. In other words, this complicated dynamic added up to irrelationship.

Ian and Danny had knocked heads repeatedly since shaking hands after signing their company's operating agreement—an agreement that Ian felt was needlessly confining while Danny felt that it allowed too much latitude and too little accountability.

About a year after the company was formed, Danny began to make a pitch for revising the operating agreement and devoting more resources to realizing their business plan. This occurred just as Ian was putting together a proposal for a new and potentially very lucrative business opportunity. He argued that this was not the moment he ought to be made to refocus his energies on Danny's concerns. This only added to Danny's anxiety about the business and his place in it, causing him to reiterate his frequent complaint that his partners didn't listen to him and undervalued his contributions.

This was not the first time Ian had ducked Danny's attempts to elicit what he believed were necessary levels of accountability and improved clarity and commitment concerning their respective responsibilities. Ian consistently downplayed this while insisting that without his creative capacity, they would have no joint project to begin with. At times he crossed into more personal territory and accused Danny of not trusting his two partners. Through all of this, Greg rarely ventured an opinion on Ian's work or Danny's concerns. The one point of agreement the three men shared was the feeling that his own work was unappreciated by the others.

Friction among the partners became serious enough to cause them to wonder if they had made a mistake deciding to work together in the first place. It even threatened to ruin valued, long-term friendships. So the partners requested a consultation with us after hearing about a successful intervention we had managed that brought about the reconciliation of antagonists in a community in crisis on the West Coast.

We met with the three men and listened as they explained their frustration with one another. Each insisted that he was doing what he believed was best for the company and each other. However, in times of particularly high stress, none of the three would lower their guard enough even to validate the importance of what the others contributed to their organization. Each admitted to increasing doubt that they could find a way to work together, and sometimes accusations of sabotage would surface. Despite this, if asked about the company's mission and work, all three indicated pride in the product they produced and cited feedback they received through electronic media. Obviously, the disconnect threatened their ability to continue working together and the survival of their company.

We agreed to work with them, especially by helping them develop a way of using the 40-20-40 and the Self-Other Assessment in a way that suited the workplace. The 40-20-40 was explained not just as a means of improving communication but also as way to validate one another's experience of working together *and* enhance individual and collective accountability.

After open discussion, the partners agreed that the most useful goal they could agree on would probably be to undercut negative feelings troubling their work together. They were able to buy into the idea that this could be done by creating a higher level of awareness of each member's contribution to their work, including their emotional investment.

Needless to say, this was a perfect fit for the 40-20-40. They followed a format of timed shares for each partner—four minutes to begin and three minutes for subsequent shares. The goal was for each member to focus on and verbalize his contribution—and his only—to the current working situation, both positive and negative. In his share, each man was permitted to take ownership and accountability for no more than 60 percent and no less than 40 percent of any issue confronting all three of them. This left a space of 20 percent in the middle for relational clarification and negotiation, that is, for working out how conflicts could be resolved without impinging on anyone else's 40 percent. The following illustrates how using the 40-20-40 affected the working relationship of the three partners.

"We still have problems," Danny said. "But it's not like it was at all. Even when we don't agree on the solutions, we're committed to how we go about finding them."

Ian remarked that even when "the bad, old ways" of doing things surfaces, he's able to step back—even when the three of them aren't together—and regroup.

"Last Sunday Danny was hitting me with emails again about the damned business plan. He gets on a tear about 'monetizing our work more effectively' that makes me crazy. I used to get so mad that I'd get into a shouting match by email! Then my wife would get mad at me because it would spoil our quiet family time because I couldn't *not* respond. Finally I walked away from the computer when you started using that 'breach of contract' language you pull out every so often."

"Yeah," Danny replied. "You've talked about how that gets to you, but it just made me angrier that you didn't answer me again after that. It was like I was just being ignored again. But I get so worked up and afraid when I can't make you guys see how much it scares me that we're not more proactive about certain things."

They met four days later with Sunday's unresolved conversation still hanging over them. As usual, Greg hadn't been directly involved in Ian and Danny's squabbles, but he was so uneasy he couldn't make eye contact with either of them when they met.

Danny wanted to know right off why Ian didn't respond to his last email.

"Actually, I wrote several responses," Ian countered, "and have learned enough not to send anything when I write something with smoke coming out of my ears."

"Well, I don't know if that was better or worse: I had trouble sleeping. I was so worried about what was going on with you, how this was going to end up."

Obviously, this scenario isn't perfect, but two aspects of this conflict illustrate the changes they made through practice of the 40-20-40: Ian was able to make the decision to walk away from an escalating situation that couldn't be managed through email; and Danny was able to admit, however guardedly, that he cared about Ian's feelings and investment in their company as well as his own.

"Stepping back, I can see what happened that Sunday morning as a chance to get a grip on our feelings about our business—the exciting part *and* the risky part," Ian reflected. "Telling each other the truth about how nervous we are makes all the difference. I'm finally getting that you hammer us with that damned business plan because you're scared: I'd thought it was just your way of trying to control everything we do."

"I know I come across as a one-way street sometimes," Danny admitted. "This isn't the first place I've heard that. But I know what I know about business, about how things work, so of course I'm afraid everything we do is going to end in wasted time and money if we don't do a better job taking care of, well, business! Yeah, without what you do, we don't have a product. But a company has to be treated like a company!"

"It makes all the difference to me when I hear you say something positive about my work. The more that sinks in the easier it is for me not to get so pissed off when I get—I know you're not going to like this—those hysterical emails!"

"Yeah. I know. I do get hysterical sometimes alone at the keyboard."

Greg had been quiet through all of this. Finally he remarked, "It's amazing how much easier it is to go through this when we tell each other we're scared."

Exercise: Cultivation of Appreciation *(Couples)*

The following practice is designed to foster mutual appreciation and gratitude. Practiced regularly, it empowers both or all participants in a relationship individually and jointly and is optimized if it's part of a couple's or group's lifestyle as opposed to being kept in reserve for times of crisis. One of its greatest benefits is that it undermines the temptation many of us feel to reduce partners (of whatever type) to adversaries during disagreements.

Take a few minutes for each of you to write down at least three times when your partner made a point of showing up for you, spontaneously did something kind or loving, or in some other way made you proud of your connection to one another.

Make a particular effort to include a recent incident, even if, at the moment, you don't particularly feel the warmth it evoked at the time. Write down in two or three sentences what happened, why it was special, and how it felt at the time.

Using the 40-20-40, take turns sharing with one another what you've written.

Exercise: Figuring Out What Works *(Couples)*

Every relationship involves negotiating how people live their lives together. Go through the following exercise together and write answers to the questions with input from both sides.

- What issues and problems (or worse) have you encountered in your life together that you've worked out successfully?
- What specific exchanges or negotiations took place that allowed that to happen?
- Have you used that type of negotiation unsuccessfully on some other issue? What do you believe are the barriers to solving it? For example, can you identify specific areas of resistance in yourself? Can you give the reason for them?

Discuss your findings in each case. The goal is not necessarily to find a solution at this moment but rather to develop an understanding of what things do and do not work for you as a couple when you encounter problems.

Exercise: Using a Chronic Issue as a Means of Empowerment (Couples)

Revisit the Chronic Issues Exercise for couples in Chapter 11, and now choose one of the issues you identified to explore further. Reflect on and answer the following questions as individuals.

- Who is negatively affected by this issue?
- What is the negative effect/harm? What is its cause? How has the harmed party used this issue to prevent resolution or aggravate other issues?
- How do you feel about the harm to your partner?
- What have you done to stop and to repair the harm? What are the results?

After you've completed your individual work on these four questions, reflect together on your answers, using the following questions as a guide.

- What emotional experience does the harm to your partner evoke in you? How does that affect your perception of the two of you as intimate partners?
- How has your partner been harmed? How do you feel about that?
- How do you view your partner's contribution to this issue? How do you feel about your partner's willingness or unwillingness to own her or his part in this issue? How do both of your feelings continue to affect this issue?

In the exercises in Chapter 11, you developed a list of steps that could be taken to repair relationship issues. Openness to this kind of sharing is the essence of interactive repair and forms the impetus for Empowerment in the DREAM Sequence.

Now you'll apply those steps to reconsider the chronic issue identified at the beginning of this exercise.

Reflect individually and then write about how those steps may apply to the chronic issue. Discuss your thoughts with your partner, using the following questions to begin creating a foundation for joint problem-solving.

- What could and should each partner be willing to do for this to work?
- How can those steps change your impasse or your perception of it?
- How can sharing this exercise create a new sense of ownership of the problem and contribute to its resolution?

Finally, using the 40-20-40, reflect on what this exercise suggests to you in terms of both individual and joint empowerment within your relationship and how this empowerment looks and feels to you compared to past experience with difficult issues.

Do Relationships Have Character?

"For most of the time we've known each other, I've pretty much blamed Max for everything that went wrong in our relationship." Angelina paused. "Then oh man! We started looking at this irrelationship stuff—how we'd made sure our lives actually let us avoid each other! We'd never thought about a relationship as something that has to be cared for—kind of like it was our child!"

Psychological defenses are survival mechanisms necessary for every healthy person's functioning. They enable us to navigate day-to-day anxieties and other challenges by diverting our awareness of, or dissociating, them. Character can be defined as the sum total of psychological defense—in other words, character is the totality of mechanisms we use to feel safe.[4]

Irrelationship is an amalgam of misused defenses that actually prevent us from entering into authentic lives. Among the consequences of this is an inability to communicate genuinely with others in a way that makes intimacy possible. A major part of that is an inability to reckon with one's own issues, fears, and personal problems—perhaps similar to what Twelve-

Step programs refer to as character defects—which leave us alienated from others. Willingness to look at those parts of ourselves is vital to developing Empowerment as understood in the DREAM Sequence.

"When I began to understand our relationship as needing care itself," Angelina commented, "that was when I started seeing how mean I was to Max and how destructive that was to our marriage. How can anything get fixed if I'm so focused on faultfinding? But in a funny way, we were enabling each other because Max always seemed totally willing to be a scapegoat."

As is the case with most of the concepts and practices in this book, Empowerment isn't a one-person job: it has to be cultivated with others. This is why it proved meaningful and useful as an aspect of the community-in-crisis intervention mentioned earlier. One of the first casualties of irrelationship is the sense of camaraderie and teamwork necessary for successful management of many aspects of our lives—personal, professional, and otherwise. Parenting, for example, by its very nature is an intimate undertaking, making it likely to bring out anyone's more unattractive characteristics. By an odd turn, those unattractive characteristics are likely to be on full display to the person with whom we are co-parenting—a person who, in our early acquaintanceship, we probably took considerable care to impress with how cool and put together we were.

Max had not found it easy to believe that his quiescence as scapegoat was actually intended to be helpful to his wife.

"That was a hard sell. Angelina was so out of control that I felt sorry for her. But keeping quiet was a way of staying out of the line of fire. Yeah, she was pretty brutal sometimes. But for whatever reason, when I looked at her face I didn't really see mean; she just looked like she was crying, or about to. It made me so sad, but I had no idea what to do about it. Her anger was like a wall. Down deep, though, I never really thought it had all that much to do with me."

"Yeah and I read that whole thing totally wrong," Angelina replied. "Your silence seemed like some kind of passive-aggressive thing, like you weren't about to agree with anything I said, so you just ignored it. It was like you were rubbing something in my face—something I totally didn't get. And that just made me even angrier. There I was, trying as hard as I could to show you how you're supposed to be in a relationship (Like I was some kind of big fat success! Ha!), but it was like you were just ignoring me. God it was infuriating."

Max honestly believed that holding his peace was the best thing he could do for his wife, even if doing so seemed to validate whatever she said or thought about their relationship. The one thing he was positive about was that he didn't want to lose their marriage. But he didn't know any other way to get that across to her other than to just accept whatever came out of her mouth. Nevertheless, the virulence of Angelina's attacks took its toll.

"A point came when my silence wasn't just acquiescence: it became outright protective. Well, that didn't demand any change in strategy because it was what I had always done. But after a while, I started to get scared. I knew it was a contradiction, the idea that saving our marriage depended on keeping you away from me. How long can you do that with somebody you love and want to be with? It worried me so much I was having trouble sleeping."

Max and Angelina's marriage had developed a critical two-way defect: a wall neither could acknowledge to the other but which made it impossible to share anything with the person they loved. In this instance, the terms *defect* and *defense* are interchangeable and are glaring markers of irrelationship. Taking inventory of ourselves using the 40-20-40 allows us to identify how we're blocking ourselves from intimacy—in short, from the reciprocal process that both creates and *is* relationship sanity. Users of the 40-20-40 can safely take ownership of their own part in whatever is going on between two (or more) people. The unexpected power of this technique is shown in how Angelina and Max transformed their marriage by simply telling the truth about their own experience, no matter how dark or frightening.

"It took a while," Angelina explained, "but we've learned how to use the things I got mad about to figure out how each of us contributed to an issue. That's a lot better than getting pissed off about the same things over and over and getting madder each time because he wouldn't fight with me. Nothing I said ever seemed to even penetrate, so nothing ever changed.

"I don't know what changed it. But listening to Max, I finally started seeing how getting angry wasn't just hurting Max: it was treating our marriage like a war game. But the last thing I wanted to do was surrender. I needed to be the one who figured out what was wrong and how to fix it. That always kept Max on the outside—didn't even let him be Max. I had to be the expert, and that was really hard to put down."

Doing the 40-20-40 was just as unnerving for Max.

"It was the last thing I wanted to do. My stealth gave me a way to be with Angelina. But when we do the 40-20-40, I'm giving that up. It means I'm telling Angelina exactly what I'm feeling. That always leads into why I do what I do, which means explaining to her why I don't fight back. Man, that's hard because then I've got nowhere left to hide, which means I'm choosing once and for all to be *with* Angelina.

"Keeping my mouth shut and letting Angelina run over me had always seemed safer than actually telling her how I felt. It was kind of a cagey way of not surrendering to her. When you do the 40-20-40, you're surrendering. Everything. Everybody is. But it's the only way to figure out what's wrong and fix it."

Irrelationship can be understood as the sum total of the character defects of the participants, who learned their defense techniques as small children in order to survive in family settings perceived by the child to be dangerous. The ultimate cost is that these techniques do not permit direct communication of anxiety and vulnerability.

"When I finally realized how far Max and I were from each other, it scared me," Angelina confessed. "I hadn't thought about it this way in a long time, but I remembered that I actually love Max and don't want to lose him. I started getting just a little inkling of what it's like for him when I'm always yelling at him. I was always telling myself that he was the bad guy because he never seemed to listen to me. And I'd say things about it even in front of company at family gatherings. Oh, my God, I'd been so *mean* trying to get him to react the way I wanted him to."

Max admitted, "There were a couple of times at your mom's house that I could have changed the equation—could have said something to keep it from getting so ugly." He paused, then continued, "I was being passive-aggressive. I let you have all the rope you wanted. I knew it was mean at the time. And it embarrassed everybody—even me—but I just let it happen. And I've hated myself for it ever since."

Waiting

Max's silence had many nuances but always included giving space to Angelina, hoping—sometimes desperately—that something would change so she would give him the space to accept and forgive her. But doing that on the sly insulated him from having to take any responsibility for whatever went wrong. This type of scenario can continue for years without either party being aware that they're growing further and further apart, though they continue to share the same bed without ever entertaining the idea of actual infidelity.

"Even when things started to change, it took a while for me to let go of judging and blaming you," Angelina revealed. "I still needed to feel superior, and framing everything bad as your fault let me stay in that groove. It was a while before I was willing for you to see, or even for *me* to see, how much I cared for you. And that made me even more afraid that you would leave me. I'd get so mad at you because, well, because everything wasn't my idea of perfect, and I told myself you were the reason it was like that. That way if everything blew up it was your fault.

"I suppose the bottom line is that the last thing I wanted to believe was that I was supposed to rely on you, that I *could* rely on you. But when I was a kid, I could never rely on my mom and dad: I had to make sure everything was okay on my own. It was a total set-up. And, wouldn't you know it, every boyfriend I ever had was a disappointment, a flake who finally just disappeared. Hell *no,* I wasn't going to just let myself depend on you!"

Identifying irrelationship often comes about when the pain of clinging to a relationship defect outweighs the fear of letting it go. Recognizing the impact our past has had in our relationships is the beginning of buying into authentic ways of giving and receiving love that grows into the possibility and reality of intimacy and growth. These are the essential ingredients for Empowerment, which is often the point when couples begin to understand what we call the us-ness of their relationship—the space in which the "you and I" give way to the "we"—and explore that "we" wherever it takes them.

Exercise: Expanding Empowerment *(Couples)*

Empowerment is established by jointly creating more effective means of communicating with each other—communication that includes both the ability to speak and the ability to hear.

Having seen how using the 40-20-40 establishes the practice of effective communication and Self-Other Assessment, you can use the following questions as a guide to explicitly understand what actually happens to you and your relationship as a result.

Because Self-Other Assessment is reciprocal, it builds Empowerment by jointly creating a space for shared acceptance, care, and affection in which both partners feel loved and lovable. As we've said elsewhere in this book, this is compassionate empathy and the set-up for relationship sanity—that state in which partners build commitment to one another by sharing openness and vulnerability.

While asking each other the questions, try to maintain focus on what your partner is really saying about being together with you instead of jumping ahead in your own mind to what you are going to say when asked the same question.

- What is it like to think about both of us having equal power and place in our relationship? What is like to make such a choice deliberately?
- What have you learned *about yourself* by being hospitable and compassionate to your partner?

- What do you think it would look like to practice this kind of hospitality, i.e., compassionate empathy, in relationships with others who are important to you?
- All of us have parts of ourselves and past experiences that we don't want to remember. What could you do to recover and accept those things as part of who you are today? How would that be empowering?
- How could that same practice be used to recover or rebuild lost parts of our relationship?
- How would our relationship change if we became comfortable with practicing that kind of honesty and openness with one another?

As a final reflection on Empowerment, return again to the Joint Compassion Meditation Exercise from Chapter 1.

- Set a time limit of three to five minutes. Sit quietly, focusing on your breath while, at the same time, taking note of the stream of thoughts passing through your mind. Remember to do this *without judgment.* Then return your attention to your breathing.
- When the time expires, write down briefly what you remember about what passed through your mind. Flag anything that may seem connected to the idea of sharing Empowerment with your partner, but remember this exercise has no right or wrong; it's simply an observation practice designed to help you understand yourself and what's happening for you as you learn about relationship sanity.

Staying on Target: Overprotected versus Empowered

Using the 40-20-40 is teaching you to create relationship sanity, which, in turn, creates space for the mutually empowering, alternative experience of Self and Self-Other as we. This is the window into interpersonal reality as it actually is: dynamic, shared, and ever-changing.

Key Takeaways

- We're learning how Self-Other—a growing sense and experience of that third entity, our *us-ness*—is the means of accessing Empowerment.
- By using the 40-20-40, we create Empowerment together as we become able to value each other and reciprocate care, acceptance, and affection.
- Using the 40-20-40 creates relationship sanity by our becoming able to give *and* receive, as well as experiencing ourselves as both loved and lovable.
- We're becoming accustomed to the idea of taking care of our relationship as a third entity, our *us-ness*, and to creating a language for doing so.
- The 40-20-40 becomes a means of Empowerment by increasing our awareness of dissociated parts of ourselves and accepting them.

Imagine what Empowerment looks and feels like as you become hospitable to blocked parts of yourselves: you're actually empowering your relationship by welcoming conflicted parts of yourselves and one another.

At times this practice is probably going to make you feel overwhelmed. The most powerful remedy for those feelings is to share them with each other. When practical, this can include returning, even briefly, to the Joint Compassion Breathing Exercise and then sharing where your feelings have taken you. This not only reduces stress but also promotes Empowerment by puncturing the illusion of self-sufficiency.

Now, once again, pause and look at each other. Then, using the free-association technique, discuss thoughts, thought fragments, feelings, reflections, and analysis of your journey on the road of relationship sanity.

Chapter 13

Alternatives

Compassionate empathy makes space for alternative experiences of ourselves as we interact with others, especially our partner or spouse. A term sometimes used for this is *deterritorialization*.[1] If we remain open to it, the hospitality to one another that this implies can continue to grow indefinitely, perhaps validating Heraclitus' observation that the only constant is change!

Creating New Shared Spaces for Effective Communication

"*God,* how I hate you!" Ava screamed as she fled to the bathroom, locking the door. Her husband Logan and their two sons, still at the dinner table, stared at the door for a moment then looked back at one another. As usual, they didn't know what to say after another reprise of this familiar scene.

After a moment, Logan, a medical doctor, rose from the table and went to the bathroom door. Calmly he tried to coax Ava to come out in a tone as cool and detached as if he were a talking to an elderly patient who refused to take her medications.

When your partner seems to blow up irrationally, the first impulse might be to take cover and ride it out—especially if you're the target. And oftentimes, that may actually be the best strategy until cooler heads prevail. But sometimes this ostensibly mature way of dealing with a crisis is a covert means of emotionally abandoning a person who makes us uneasy because we're afraid the person is asking for something we're not sure we can or want to offer.

Half an hour later, Logan sent their sons as emissaries to the bathroom door, hoping the fear in their voices would persuade their mother to capitulate and just let things return to normal. Logan then approached the bathroom door.

"Please, Ava," he said calmly. "This isn't good for anybody. The boys are upset, and I don't get what's happening. Just come out and we can talk."

"You're driving me crazy!" Ava stage-whispered from the other side of the door.

"I—What? What are you talking about? Are we just going to go back on everything we've worked on? What happened? In the last two days, you've been all over me, telling me how grandiose I am, I'm entitled, and I don't show up for you and the boys, all just out of the blue. I dunno *what* it is! What did I do? When?"

After working on their irrelationship isolation routine for some months, Ava and Logan had made major progress in how they listened and related to one another after having nearly divorced a couple years earlier. But they still had occasional blow-ups, which Logan at first blamed on his wife's unpredictability. But after taking a little time to reflect, he'd begun to become more honest about his part in her frustration when he unconsciously redeployed his under-the-radar distancing and denying by being late picking up the boys for their martial arts class or by forgetting to run errands Ava requested. At first, Logan would write these lapses off (to himself) as meaningless, or small stuff. But Ava didn't buy it: she had lived with Logan long enough to recognize it, even if Logan didn't.

"Just come out, Ava," Logan calmly persisted. "I know I've hurt you somehow and I want to understand, but right now I don't."

"Of course you don't—you *never* do," Ava muttered with disgust as she opened the door.

Ava and Logan first started practicing Self-Other Assessment when they decided to try counseling instead of a divorce lawyer. So they knew irrelationship and the 40-20-40 drill very well: they began a cycle of timed shares in which each took her or his own personal inventory, including their experience of the other and their accompanying and subsequent feelings as well as how each perceived the current crisis. In addition to owning up to their own part, each party suggested possible solutions and said what they thought they contributed to what's going right in their relationship— especially when problems arise. Little by little, they learned, in alternating three-minute shares, to reveal their own feelings without finger-pointing, shaming, or punishing the other. This time, however, it didn't go quite the way it usually did.

"I want you to start," said Ava.

"Okay. Well—like I said, I don't know what I've done . . .," began Logan.

"Already you're blaming me, Logan—not by what you say but what you're leaving out—for whatever reason, since you usually don't have any trouble rubbing things in my face," Ava almost screamed.

Suddenly boiling over, Logan began shouting. "I do everything for you, Ava! You *and* the kids. Remember how hard it was to arrange my work hours so I could be with the boys two afternoons a week? And who's making all the money? Who arranges everywhere we go, everything we do? *I* do. Do you ever say thank—"

"Back to that—*again*," Ava hissed. "'Hey Ava! Look at *me!* Look at *me!* I do *everything* and what do *you* do?' Nothing I do cuts any ice with you, Logan, you're so busy congratulating yourself on how generous you are!"

Logan just glared back.

"Does it ever occur to you what it feels like when you compare yourself to me—the stay-at-home mom? You *know* it hurts my feelings, but whenever I try to talk about it, you're not in the mood, or you're not in that head at that moment, so you just brush it off! Brush it off because everything you do for me is supposed to make *me* feel *better!* Your whole attitude is as if I were one of your patients—only today, I'm a non-compliant patient! How does it feel that you can't force me to make *you* feel better?"

For a moment, Logan gaped at Ava. Finally he managed to say, "I really never—I never thought of it like that," and was silent.

"Well, it's old news to me, Logan," Ava fired back, "folding your arms across your chest and congratulating yourself. If you ever bother to notice my feelings are hurt, you can always just remind yourself how much you do for Ava and the boys. Pfft! I know it from memory, Logan. And you think I don't notice the pissed off look you get on your face when I don't stay with the script? And it isn't just me, Logan: even the boys have started learning how they're supposed to act, what they're supposed to say to make sure Daddy's happy!"

Even couples with a lot of practice at Self-Other Assessment can relapse into old performance routines—usually, but not always, when the couple's lifestyle makes it difficult for them to build shared downtime into their lives—downtime they can use to refresh the connection they've built using the 40-20-40. Such lapses aren't usually anyone's fault: the natural demands of taking care of a household, especially one with small children, can make the time needed for a pause seem scarce. Little by little, things can go awry without anyone realizing it until the couple's connection has gotten so off-kilter that a blowup seems to break in from out of nowhere. This is what happened to Ava and Logan.

The backstory is that Logan's long working hours increased the isolation Ava often felt when left alone with the kids. Logan felt guilty about this but consoled himself by frequently reminding himself how much he does for his family—mostly through expensive family activities, children's entertainment, martial arts school, and exotic vacations. At the same time, he avoided discussing family finances with Ava, which made her feel even more on the outside. In short, Ava and Logan slipped back into the bad, old ways of their song-and-dance routine: Logan preened himself on being a great caretaker, while largely ignoring how taxing being a stay-at-home mom was for Ava. Moreover, he felt entitled to be proud of how hard he worked to take care of his family, so it grated on him when Ava didn't seem as appreciative as he felt she ought to be.

After her tirade, Ava became uneasy as she generally did when she disclosed her feelings. In response, instead of holding to onto her 40 percent, she compensated by withdrawing too far into her side of the 40-20-40, which opened the way for Logan to feel that his caretaking was necessary because of how badly she needed his help. This by itself was an incursion into Ava's 40-percent zone, but enlisting the kids to cajole Ava out of the bathroom was worse. Finally hiding his vulnerability behind his detached clinical demeanor—a technique he'd used earlier in their marriage—caused Ava to start having thoughts of divorce again.

"Ava, have you said everything you need to say?"

"What, now you're going to criticize me for not doing that 40-20-40 thing right?"

"No, not you, me," Logan admitted. "I'm doing it again: I slipped right back into 'fix you' mode instead of listening to you. Our old song-and-dance routine. It was gross. I'm so sorry, Ava. Maybe we can start the 40-20-40 over again. I'll start if you want."

Ava paused, sighed, and then said quietly, "You already did."

Exercise: Avoiding Mutually Assured Destruction *(Couples)*

By now it should be fairly clear that relationship sanity is brought about by the healing created by interactive repair and empowers both parties by making space for alternative ways of treating relationship issues. This, of course, adds up to Mutuality, the culmination of the DREAM Sequence.

This exercise gives you insight into common pitfalls as you learn new ways of sharing communication and vulnerability. It also helps couples to see serious conflicts as opportunities for collaborating, so they can develop Alternatives to habitual styles of relating that usually hit a wall and deepen isolation.

Before we go into the exercise, however, we encourage you to read and reflect on the two following models that illuminate blocked communication and destructive behavior. Any single point made in either model may reveal an opportunity for you to pivot from accustomed behaviors into creative Alternatives.

Julie and John Gottman describe four characteristics of relationships in serious trouble—characteristics that they refer to as the Four Horsemen of the Apocalypse.[2] If the Horsemen remain unchallenged, the relationship is probably doomed. The Four Horsemen are as follows.

1. **Criticism:** This is not just criticism of discrete traits or behaviors but global criticism penetrating the character and personality of its target. Criticism is global. It attacks the mate's character or personality. The following illustrates the difference between criticism and a complaint: *Complaint:* "The car is out of gas. I'm annoyed that you said you'd get gas but didn't." *Criticism:* "You didn't get gas again! You can't be relied on for anything!"

2. **Contempt:** Contempt can be seen in a set of behaviors directed at someone that communicate *disgust*. It includes but is not limited to sneering, sarcasm, name-calling, eye rolling, mockery, hostile humor, and condescension. Contempt is primarily transmitted nonverbally. It does not signal any interest in reconciliation but instead maintains disrespectful behaviors that abet conflict and ill feeling on both sides. Research has shown a higher incidence of illness and disease in couples with ongoing contempt for one another than among couples that practice respect for each other.

3. **Defensiveness:** Defensive behaviors convey the message, "The problem isn't me—it's *you*." From this position, the implication is that because your partner threw the first stone, she or he is responsible for the entire conflict. Rather than taking responsibility for your own behavior, you point to something she or he did before complaining about you, thus you sidestep validating the idea that your partner may have a legitimate complaint or that you play any role in your conflicts with one another.

4. **Stonewalling:** Stonewalling develops in relationships where intense arguments break out suddenly and ongoing criticism and contempt lead to increasing levels of defensiveness until one partner begins turning away. The stonewaller acts as if he—research

indicates that 85 percent of stonewallers are male—doesn't care what his partner says or does. In short, he manages conflict by disengaging and turning away from it—sometimes going so far as to turn away from the relationship itself.

Thomas Gordon has outlined twelve communication roadblocks that he refers to as the Dirty Dozen.[3] An example is provided with each roadblock.

1. **Ordering, Directing:** "Stop feeling sorry for yourself!"
2. **Warning, Threatening:** "You'll never make friends if you don't . . ." or "You'd better stop worrying so much or . . ."
3. **Moralizing, Preaching:** "Life isn't a bowl of cherries, you know!" or "You shouldn't feel that way." or "You need to learn some patience."
4. **Advising, Giving Solutions:** "What you should do is . . ." or "I don't understand why you haven't . . ." or "The way to handle this is by . . ."
5. **Persuading with Logic, Arguing:** "Here's what's wrong with how you see this issue . . ." or "The fact is . . ." or "Well, yeah, but . . ."
6. **Judging, Criticizing, Blaming:** "You're thinking like a child." or "You're just lazy." or "What did you do to make him angry?"
7. **Praising, Agreeing:** "Well, I think you're doing a *great* job!" or "You're right! That teacher sounds *awful*."
8. **Name-calling, Ridiculing:** "What a crybaby!" or "I can't believe you're worked up about not getting an A."
9. **Analyzing, Diagnosing:** "You know what's wrong with you? You're . . ." or "Ah, you're just tired." or "What you're really trying to say is . . ." or "What's wrong with you?"
10. **Reassuring, Sympathizing:** "Don't worry—it'll be fine." or "You'll feel better when all this is over." or "Ah, c'mon! Cheer up!"
11. **Questioning, Probing:** "Why did you do that?" or "Who said that? Who told you that?" or "What did you think would happen?" or "How did you . . .?"

12. **Diverting, Sarcasm, Withdrawal:** "Let's talk about something more pleasant, shall we?" or "Why don't *you* tell them how it should be done?" (Spoken while the speaker's attention obviously seems focused elsewhere.)

Now for the exercise. This is an opportunity to reflect on the behaviors explained in the two models and compare them to your own experience. You may even be able to recall and add behaviors of your own that you realize you've used to keep your distance from others.

Take a good, hard look at how your disagreements descend into sometimes dragged out fights loaded with infliction of pain and retaliation. Calling these tactics by their names will help you catch them early and head them off before they become full-on battles with no holds barred.

Agreeing jointly to use this "early warning system" not only allows you to make better choices when treating relationship issues, but sticking to this agreed-upon process will build trust. With practice, you'll even begin to view conflict as a vital part of intimacy.

Think about arguments you have or have had that turn into big fights. As you review, identify and write down two or three recurring patterns in your interactions that lead to negative outcomes. Some of these outcomes may be glaring while others may be subtler but stretch out over a period of days or longer.

On the basis of what you've learned about relationship sanity, write down three alternative behaviors or strategies for each of the recurring patterns that you listed. These should be Alternatives you could have chosen that could at least potentially have led to a more satisfying outcome *for both of you.*

Exercise: Solo Activity for Each Partner *(Individuals)*

Return to the issue that you've been working through in the Repair and the Empower stages of the DREAM Sequence.

The following exercise assesses the effectiveness of your process for resolving the issue and your progress to date. Each of the following items highlights turning points as well as typical sticking points in problem-solving. Write down your responses individually.

- After reviewing the work you've done to date on this issue, write down how your perception of the causes of this issue has changed.
- What harm has it caused and to whom? How have you justified your part in the harm or justified *ignoring* your part?
- What feelings do you have about the harm caused? How does it feel to be sharing a process of repairing this issue? How does it feel to let go of isolating and destructive behaviors?
- In light of your contribution to this issue, what advice would you give to others to help them find alternative ways to deal with relationship problems?

When ready, share your answers with one another.
- How has this issue affected the connection between us?
- In what specific ways has the issue harmed our relationship? How can we use the harms each of us identified to create compassionate empathy for each other? How can we use these harms as cues for taking better care of our relationship—our us-ness?
- What feelings do each of us have about learning practical, new ways of taking care of our relationship?
- What guidelines can we put in place to help us to *sustain* these new ways of addressing relationship issues?

Exercise: Moving Toward Alternatives *(Couples)*

Solutions related to interactive repair as developed in the last few chapters easily morph into techniques for realizing shared empowerment. Such empowerment is a natural outgrowth of the connection that results from practicing compassionate empathy, that is, practicing openness to hearing and understanding the experience of your partner. Relationship sanity can't develop apart from this type of deliberate shared connection.

The following exercise uses the work you've done on your chosen issue up to this point in order to expand your practice of creating Alternatives for managing relationship bumps and disasters.

As you reflect on your experience thus far, write down your individual responses to the following questions.

- What is it like to consider the way you've handled conflict in the past isn't the way it has to be in the future?
- What would an alternative solution look like when treating a real-life day-to-day problem?
- What impact do you think practicing this alternative would have on your us-ness, i.e., on the discrete entity that is your relationship?
- What comes up for you when you consider the idea of replacing polarizing arguments with a process of jointly creating solutions?
- How does that prospect change your overall perception of your connection with your partner?
- Finally, conduct a 40-20-40 of timed shares in which you disclose to one another your responses to the previous questions.

An outcome of the Empowerment phase of the DREAM Sequence is growth of role flexibility. This includes openness to alternative ways of experiencing Self-Other. In the context of irrelationship, even experience itself is novel, since the defensive routines of irrelationship are designed to maintain a safe, detached sameness. The techniques of self-disclosure embodied in the 40-20-40 are the catalyst for this alternative mode of being in a relationship and how they improve the sense of joint ownership of all that happens in the relationship—good, bad, pleasant or not, desirable, or repellant. In every event, this ownership creates consciousness in invested parties so that they can safely deploy ways of being together that promote illimitable and exciting new experiences of self and other.

Exercise: Using Compassionate Empathy to Develop Alternatives (*Individuals*)

The following practice is designed to be done individually rather than jointly as a couple. Sharing the outcome will probably be of mutual interest but isn't necessary to appreciate the exercise's outcome and benefits.

Recall a situation in which someone clearly wronged you but without causing serious harm.

- What feelings would come up for you if someone were to suggest that you attempt to view that person with empathy?
- Considering what you've experienced in earlier exercises, what can you imagine happening if you decided to put aside your victim role and the resentment that goes with it?
- What thoughts and feelings come up if you try to empathize with the person who wronged you?
- What connection can you see between accepting yourself as you really are and attempting to empathize with that person?
- Reflect on the connection between intimacy and accepting others unconditionally *as they are.* You may want to write down some notes about this.

The bottom line of this practice is that it provides an opportunity for imagining Self-Other experience *outside* a close relationship. This expands the frame of reference for the power of the Alternatives stage of the DREAM Sequence.

Exercise: Compassionate Empathy as Catalyst of Alternatives (Couples)

The following exercise is designed to help partners to return to a place of safety with one another when the anxiety connected to the relationship sanity process becomes distracting or even overwhelming.

Sit quietly with one another and allow yourselves to settle into the moment while recalling the vulnerability to one another that you've been exposing and cultivating. Remind yourselves that even in your openness and vulnerability you're safe with each other.

Now expand that idea of safety to include the world in which you live your everyday life: your neighborhood, workplace, and community. Consider the possibility that an excitement similar to what you are developing in your relationship can be created elsewhere in your life, including in new and unexpected places—that, in fact, new alternatives are possible in every part of your life.

Remind yourself that your partner is doing this exercise *with you*—that you're recreating your relationship *together*. Imagine this recreation as an alternative space for sharing unconditional hospitality and compassionate empathy for one another.

Now refocus your attention on the two of you but not as individuals sitting in separate chairs. Instead, without applying each other's names or other monikers, wordlessly visualize yourselves as sharing the experience of "together" in every setting, in every part of your lives, regardless of whether or not you're in each other's immediate presence.

Exercise: Final Reflection on Alternatives

Return to the practice of observing your thoughts, this time to gauge the impact, conscious or not, of the idea of creating Alternatives. The work in this chapter has been directed primarily at relinquishing postures from which it was easy to accuse, blame, and even sideline our partners (and others) when we feel anxious or threatened.

As noted in earlier chapters, observing our thoughts as nonjudgmental spectators doesn't come easily to most of us. But making the deliberate attempt can accustom our minds to allowing access to information that we've kept at a distance—information vital to making better choices for ourselves.

- After setting a timer in the way you usually do, sit quietly with attention on your breath while observing the stream of thoughts passing through your mind. Then return your attention to your breath.
- Remember this exercise is not a contest to see who gets it right or who does better than whom: its purpose is to learn about how your mind is responding to new ideas, practices, and challenges.
- After your session, make notes about how it felt to be left with your own thoughts, what thoughts ran through your mind, what your reaction is to them, and how your thoughts relate to the movement you're making outside of old comfort zones.
- Conduct a 40-20-40 about this experience, using your timed shares to reveal the thoughts that surfaced during your practice.
- Take special care to reveal thoughts that cause anxiety in either or both of you and give unconditional space and hospitality to them.

Staying on Target: Knowing the Way versus Developing Alternatives

Like compassionate empathy and intimacy, Alternatives to irrelationship are co-created. Having broken free of irrelationship, shared Empowerment enables you to deliberately create alternative techniques for managing relationship stressors and anxieties—techniques that, themselves, continue to build intimacy.

Key Takeaways

- We accept the possibility that our thoughts and feelings about life and other people can be changed.
- We implement the Self-Other Assessment and 40-20-40 technique for managing anxiety, fear, anger, and conflict.
- We are beginning to see concrete examples of how our behavior can change—and are deliberately starting to change it.
- We have expanded our willingness and vision for change and growth.

Role flexibility is another of the Alternatives that Empowerment allows us to realize and grows directly out of learning the habit of using the 40-20-40. Accessing this increased sense of awareness and ownership of your contributions—good, bad, and everything in-between—directly disempowers the ways that, in the past, you've habitually used to ward off the novel or unpredictable experience of yourself and others.

Another benefit of this change is that it allows you to see and feel the difference between burnout and the sustainable empathy that builds synergy between you and those who are important to you. It transforms your perceptions of relationships so that they're no longer feared as costly and demanding but welcomed as renewing and renewable gifts given to one another.

From this new perspective, how does it feel to consider showing empathy to someone who has victimized you? Can you bring yourself to view this as an opportunity for all parties involved to feel energized instead of stuck in old roles and resentments? If you can accept yourself as you are, perhaps even your most bitterly adversarial relationships can be transformed into opportunities for building compassionate empathy—maybe even intimacy. This is the point of embracing Alternatives.

Now, looking at one another, again use free-association to discuss thoughts and thought fragments, feelings, and reflections about where you've been and where you're heading as individuals and as a couple on the road to relationship sanity.

Chapter 14

Mutuality

Mutuality is the technique, the purpose, and the culmination of relationship sanity. All the work in this book is directed at becoming able to value one another without a construct or overlay of inequality or feelings of inequality. In Mutuality, we give and receive love, caring, and trust with unconditional acceptance without giving in to the temptation to downplay or devalue our partner when we're feeling anxious about our needs or our position in the relationship. When we make mistakes—even huge blunders that sometimes destroy relationships—relationship sanity provides space to fail, get back up, and try again, all without a fear of being made to pay for our failures forever. Relationship sanity is messy because life often *is* messy. It's painful and costly because pretty much everything worth having requires putting aside our immediate wants. However, having read up to this point, you've already gotten the message that how things *were* is far less desirable than the pain and the messiness of relationship sanity.

Let's briefly revisit the phases of dependence identified by Carnes, Laaser, and Laaser, which appeared in the Introduction.[1] In the process of developing a sense of ourselves in the context of relationship, we generally develop a sense of identity by passing through phases of dependency; that is, from our life experience, we infer how much we can depend on others for help when we need it.

1. **Dependence:** We need and want help.
2. **Counterdependence:** We need help but resist it.
3. **Independence:** We're self-sufficient and don't need help.
4. **Interdependence:** We're able to give and receive help.

By these definitions, interdependence can be seen as, perhaps, the most consequential component of relationship sanity. Irrelationship is its opposite. The parties invested in irrelationship have unconsciously made a decision to step away from relationship sanity, choosing instead to act out their intimacy-related anxiety through a process psychoanalysts call *enactment*. In irrelationship terms, the enactment is the song-and-dance routine that partners use to protect themselves from getting too close by enacting one or more of the GRAFTS behaviors. These behaviors look a lot like Carnes, Laaser, and Laaser's first three phases of dependence and are a way of blocking, or dissociating, our need for help from others, especially from a would-be intimate partner. Conversely, the path of relationship sanity is a process of reassociating our feelings of anxiety and our need for others.

Compassionate empathy creates the mutual acceptance that allows balanced giving and taking, caregiving and accepting care, and loving and being loved—in other words, Mutuality. The hallmark of relationship sanity is the continually-maturing product that is Mutuality, which is the natural outcome of sustained use of the 40-20-40, the Self-Other Assessment.

Exercise: Interdependence and Relationship Sanity *(Individuals)*

Healthy interdependence is an essential part of relationship sanity. To break with irrelationship and deliberately build relationship sanity, we need to understand how we learned our own individual pattern of depending and not depending on others for support. As fleshed out in Chapter 2, our particular irrelationship song-and-dance routine is an outgrowth of how we were treated by our primary caregiver(s) as small children.

The following is an individual exercise that is designed to examine your relationships with the people most likely to have had a significant impact on you as a child and how they were present, as well as how they were absent. Either can drive a child's willingness to disclose or conceal the need for help. That pattern of willingness or unwillingness is usually taken with you into adulthood and shows how willing you are to be candid about your vulnerability and ability to rely on others.

Below is a list of persons who are often or usually the most consequential in a child's life.

- Parents/Primary caregivers
- Siblings/Other family members
- Teachers
- Friends
- Employers and coworkers
- Other adults

Make notes about how each affected your willingness to let others see your feelings, especially negative feelings, such as anger or sadness, and to ask for help when you needed it. Include how you remember each person responding or reacting when you made mistakes or otherwise did something wrong. Were they patient? Critical? Were they helpful and supportive as you learned to correct mistakes, or did they do and say things that made you feel bad?

In your notes, include specific feelings and experiences that you associate with everyone on the list. The persons suggested on the list may not include everyone who had a significant effect on you as a child, so add to your list as appropriate.

Finally, for each person, say something about the impact your interactions with that person had on you in the longer term, perhaps even up to today.

After completing your writing, take turns sharing your answers with your partner.

Exercise: Attitudes Toward Accepting Care from Others (*Individuals*)

Our ability to care and be cared for is shaped one relationship at a time, over several years. Similarly, clearing away old habits of isolation to make space for Mutuality will take time. But each change and breakthrough will feel like you're putting down a burden and is likely to make you breathe a sigh of relief.

Experiencing others' care for you is liable to expose uncomfortable attitudes and feelings that many of us feel a need to keep under wraps. Nevertheless, being able to name and clarify those attitudes is an important piece of building relationship sanity. The following exercise will help.

Our attitudes toward giving and receiving care fall broadly into several categories:

- **Quid pro quo:** I provide care with the implicit or explicit understanding that I'm entitled to expect repayment.
- **Nonemotionally-involved care:** care that does not involve any kind of personal connection. Such care may be provided by professional caregivers or may be between people who know each other but avoid emotional investment in one another.
- **Care involving exaggerated personal or emotional investment:** caretaking administered in an essentially (or apparently) one-way transaction that doesn't take into account the authentic needs of either person involved.
- **Minimal care:** caretaking, sometimes entirely impersonal, that's usually administered out of a sense of obligation and may be accompanied by feelings of guilt, resentment, or other negative emotions. Meanwhile, the person targeted by the caretaking experiences little to no benefit and may even be unaware that it's occurring.
- **Accepting care:** Caregiver and recipient authentically and unconditionally accept their respective roles vis-à-vis one another and are able to maintain openness to changes in their roles.

Now write about experiences of caregiving that have involved you as giver or receiver, or that you have observed in others. Don't worry about whether or not your scenarios seem to correspond to these five categories.

Many of us have, in the past, experienced care given by others that has conditioned or even interfered with our ability to accept care and services we need in our lives today. This can include anything from care needed during convalescence from illness to emotional support during a life crisis to requiring government services after losing a job.

Now write about experiences from your own life in which you needed the support of other people or service agencies. What happened leading to your needing those supports? What was it like for you to be in that position?

Looking back over your life, especially early childhood, reflect on and write about experiences you had with two or three caregivers.

- Which of their personal qualities had an impact on your experience of having them take care of you?
- What common characteristics do you see among these people?
- Can you recall instances in which the manner that others offered care or assistance made you hesitant or uneasy about revealing your need or willingness to accept their help?

Now repeat the exercise using the same questions, but this time look at a caretaking experience you had with someone who is either part of your life currently or someone you were connected with only temporarily or briefly. It may be a romantic interest, a caregiving professional, or even a casual acquaintance who did you a favor.

Reflect on and write about personal qualities this individual brought to your interactions and how you felt about that person in the course of your acquaintance.

From this exercise, you can glean a lot of information about what it's like for you to need and either accept or reject the assistance of caregivers within and outside your intimate circle. Discuss your findings with your partner with an eye toward identifying common or complementary experiences using the same questions.

- Which of their personal qualities do you recall having an impact on your experience of them taking care of you?
- What common characteristics do you see among these people?
- Can you see instances in which the manner that others offered services made you hesitant or uneasy about revealing your need for care?

Taking Stock

The previous exercises elucidate what it's like for you to be in the orbit of another person while taking care that you don't come close enough to allow meaningful interaction. The exercises also help explain why we manage connection with others so cautiously, as well as helping us to understand that the price we pay for keeping ourselves so safe is the forfeiture of meaningful connection and healthy interdependence.

In sane relationships, loving and being loved is a free, open dynamic between people. In irrelationship, however, loving and being loved, or, more accurately, giving and receiving caretaking, are deliberately constructed roles used as walls to keep out unscripted, spontaneous connection with others. If we're confronted with the real possibility of open, dynamic caring, many of us are unable to resolve the conflict between the need for genuine connection and the need to keep ourselves safe.

This scenario is equally true for the caretaker as for the person on whom her or his energies are spent: continually giving without allowing the recipient to respond or reciprocate is as much a protective wall as the one created by the person who refuses to allow others to care for her or him. When repeatedly rebuffed, the would-be caretaker is likely to become resentful, angry, and even contemptuous of those who refuse to validate what a great person she or he is. In either event, both parties are living in hardened silos designed to be impregnable against the threat of love and the vulnerability that comes with it. Astonishingly, some couples actually live in loneliness and isolation *within* relationships configured along such lines for years or decades.

Straitjacket No More

One day during therapy, Alexa asked wistfully, "Now that it's over, do you think I'm going to be alone for the rest of my life?"

Alexa, a savvy, attractive middle-aged woman had just broken up with a man who was fifteen years younger than herself.

"I doubt it," her therapist answered. "Too many wounded guys out there want exactly what you offer: help with their lives with no strings attached. No intimacy, no expectations, and no heavy-duty demands—in fact, no demands at all."

"Is that really what's going on?" Alexa asked, her voice trembling.

"Are you kidding? It's all that's been going on in your so-called relationships since you've been coming to me! You control the guys you date by insisting on doing all the giving. And that's what makes it entirely reasonable for you to be the one who calls all the shots about everything that happens between you—including how close you'll let him get and when. Even the sex has almost nothing to do with actually getting closer, as far as I can tell. And that's a good way to keep a guy from getting *too* important to you. You keep that nice, safe distance, and neither of you has to know how deep your feelings are—and how that scares you."

Intelligent as she was, Alexa was surprisingly naïve about her own feelings, and not just about men, but about pretty much anything. Although it smarted a bit each time one of her relationships unraveled, she actually felt even more relieved, though she wasn't about to admit that to herself. Instead, the therapy session following each breakup was spent complaining about how she keeps picking the wrong kind of guy.

Alexa's consistent pattern in her so-called relationships was to connect only with men looking for a caretaker rather than a partner. So, naturally, she consistently found herself with men who, at least for a while, were willing to play the Audience to her caretaking role, until they grew tired of being kept out of any decision-making in the relationship. So her repeatedly getting involved with the wrong kind of guy was actually her strategy for protecting herself from intimacy-related anxiety. But she came by this strategy honestly.

As a small child, Alexa took on the role of making her depressed mother feel better, although, ironically, her mother's depression was the result of her lack of success at making her daughter feel secure. Thus began the song-and-dance routine Alexa shared with her mother: Alexa was a precocious child who was able to make her mother feel that she, Alexa, was self-sufficient as well as clever enough to find ways of changing her mother's mood, or, at least, making her laugh. When her mom's mood seemed to lift, she was better able to attend to Alexa's needs, which lessened Alexa's anxiety. An added benefit for Alexa was that she came to believe in her own ability to make herself more comfortable by manipulating and controlling her environment. The downside was that she had to be constantly vigilant to make sure that she *kept* things under control.

As an adult, Alexa took her song-and-dance routine into virtually every type of relationship in her life, but it was especially consequential in would-be intimate relationships. Her self-protectiveness became a straitjacket in which she sought to fit herself and her boyfriends, so she wouldn't feel any emotional vulnerability that's a normal part of getting close to another person. Then Dylan showed up, and her therapy abruptly changed directions.

"I've never been with a man who wasn't, well, mostly absent. But Dylan—I don't know what to do with him—how to even talk to him! At first I thought I could do this. But he really wants to *know* me! He asks me about *myself* as if he's interested in, well, *me*—what I think, what I care about, what makes me nervous about dating—things I never talked about with anyone, boyfriend or not! It's so different. I can already tell he's not the guy to just let me decide all the whens and wheres of what we do together. He knows I like him, but he's already picked up that I'm not a hundred percent comfortable—and it's okay with him: he just keeps calling and showing up."

Will Alexa find her way out of her irrelationship pattern and into relationship sanity?

What's Driving Compulsive Caregiving?

As noted earlier, compulsive caregiving develops out of a child-caregiver role-reversal in which the child becomes caretaker for her primary caregiver. Ultimately, this pattern, once established, is carried forward into adulthood and applied unconsciously to any and all types of relationships.

Some of the unstated, and often unknown, rules of compulsive caregiving require ignoring and repressing pain. This was the case for Alexa, who learned early on the "never ask for anything" rule in order to avoid placing any demands on her mother. This was as much a part of her Performer role as were her precociousness and apparent self-sufficiency. But it all added up to her being a human antidepressant for her mother. And because it was apparently successful, Alexa carried the role over into her relationships with others, especially would-be romantic relationships: she felt compelled to make boyfriends feel better, regardless of their actual needs or emotional state; although as her therapist shrewdly observed, she had a knack for finding men who were looking for just such a caretaker (this is why Dylan was such a curveball). Playing those roles was how Alexa had controlled her world and kept things from falling apart—especially her own sense of safety—since she was a small child. She had no developed aptitude for relating to a boyfriend in any other way.

For his part, Dylan had been forced into deluding himself into believing that his parents could do no wrong. As an adult, however, he'd begun to realize how neglectful his mother and father were, preoccupied as they were by their own unhappy relationship; and he began to confront the impact this had had on his relationships with others. An outcome of this was that he learned that give-and-take is a normal part of any sane, adult relationship and a vital ingredient of true intimacy. He now wanted to put behind him the isolation forced on him by pretending everything was okay—that is, by playing the amused Audience. His relationship with his parents had, in fact, left him feeling angry and ignored. He was now looking for connection, love, and intimacy.

Alexa's mother's depressed mood drove Alexa to take on the task of cheering her up. As Dylan's parent's marriage went on the rocks, he created an "I'm okay, I can take care of myself" performance routine that allowed him to keep his distance from his own fear as well as the acted out rage his mother and father spent on each other. This included Dylan's taking on self-care tasks inappropriate for a small child. In response to his father's failure to provide a stable household environment, Dylan suppressed his need for an adult on whom he could rely to keep him safe and instead let his father off the hook by allowing him to believe that what care he could supply was as much as Dylan needed.

Obviously, Dylan and Alexa's caretaking routines could have intersected dangerously and led to yet another disappointing "wrong kind of guy" experience for Alexa or a reprise of Dylan's experience with parents who were unable to be present authentically for their son.

Building Relationship Sanity

Alexa's interest in a man all but required him to be willing to bow to whatever she determined was good for him and allow her to administer her caretaking as she saw fit. She had never reflected on what she actually wanted *from* a man beyond his acquiescence.

But Dylan was a game-changer. Unwilling to be put off easily or contorted into a role that didn't fit, he was clear with Alexa from the start that he was interested in *her*—not what she could do or give him to solve his problems or to make him feel better—but who she was, what *she* was interested in. And he took this so far as to actually ask questions that showed he really wanted to know about her.

Alexa's first reaction was near panic. She felt, rather than knew, that if she didn't get rid of Dylan, her accustomed way of life generally, and treating men particularly, would be jeopardized. Fortunately for her, the work she had been doing in therapy had begun to expose both her role-playing and the history driving it. Or, to put it another way, she now knew too much to simply dismiss Dylan as a poor match; plus she knew her therapist wouldn't let her get away with the excuse that Dylan was too scary. Moreover, she'd pretty much swallowed the bitter pill that her way with men was not only absurd and delusional but—and this was the kicker—the way *she* treated men is what was keeping her isolated and lonely. She had even begun to understand that her need to control romantic relationships was a leftover from her childhood survival pattern.

In time, Alexa's therapy showed her how badly her anxiety about intimacy was causing her to treat herself. This, however, didn't immediately explain her feelings for and about Dylan or fully explain how she'd treated men she'd known in the past. More time would pass before she realized that her anxiety and other feelings, sidelined since childhood, were the reason why she denied herself the excitement and the challenges of intimacy.

What Happened to Dylan?

From earlier relationships, Dylan had learned about romantic partnerships that involved the Performer/Audience roles—relationships in which the caretaker expected the target of the caretaking—himself—to reassure her that her caretaking was effective or fixed him.

Like Alexa, however, Dylan had come to realize that the role of Audience left him frustrated and lonely with no sense of sharing life-experience with another person. After several such busts, Dylan realized he didn't need to be fixed. From the time he was able to let that sink in, he made a conscious determination to never be cast in that kind of role again.

Role-play: Alexa and Dylan

Alexa discovered that she unconsciously but deliberately chose men who needed fixing. As a rescuer, fixer, or helper, she was on the lookout for men who would be the Audience for her Performer role. In return, she expected the men who she was involved with to acquiesce to her need to be needed by accepting and appearing grateful for the solutions she devised for their problems. Her partner was also expected to let her know that, thanks to her ministrations, he felt better about himself and his life.

Both parties are highly invested in maintaining this song-and-dance-routine. Designing and stepping into the song-and-dance begins at the couple's first encounter with one another. Each has learned over time to listen for certain cues when they meet someone new. If the right cues are given and received, the first conversation becomes an opportunity for scoping each other out as a potential "dance partner." If this initial contact provides sufficient reason for each to believe the other may be useful in meeting their needs, a silent contract is initiated based on the Performer-Audience paradigm. An irrelationship song-and-dance routine is born.

The participants appear at first to have different roles—one active, one passive—however, they're equally invested in creating a routine in which they feel safe. This careful scripting disallows spontaneity, unpredictability, or deviation from agreed-upon roles. Any infraction or deviation from roles would likely by viewed as betrayal, possibly warranting termination.

The anxiety-driven irrelationship dates from a person's earliest years, and, without intervention, doesn't diminish over time. Ultimately, both Alexa and Dylan figured out the isolation created by their song-and-dance routines was a higher price than either were willing to pay.

Alexa Chooses to Work *with* Instead of *on* Her Partner

Insight into past relationships finally motivated Alexa to take a risk. She could see in Dylan an opportunity to change and felt a release of tension when she consciously chose to give it a try. This soon translated into a new willingness to share experience: Alexa invited Dylan to try the 40-20-40 as she began to develop a sense of life as something shared rather something they do to or for one another.

The sheer novelty made it daunting at first. Alexa's old alarm system warned her constantly against letting Dylan get too close. But over time, his openness to her and his willingness to tell her about himself undercut those old alarms. They came to feel that they could safely tell one another about feelings around past romantic relationships and even about their experiences as children. Simply sharing those things aloud was strangely empowering for both and gave them real hope that the way things had always been wasn't how they always had to be.

Alexa had also learned in therapy that the only real way of dealing with anxiety is to look it in the face and keep walking. Sharing the truth about her fear with Dylan and then, in his turn, hearing him come clean about his own apprehension, blunted a lot of her apprehension, making it possible to go further with each share. She even began to realize that telling the truth about herself didn't jeopardize her survival, and it made her feel lighter and lighter, and closer and closer to Dylan. This, they later learned, is compassionate empathy in action and creates relationship sanity.

Though the 40-20-40 process is simple, partners seldom find it easy to adopt without resistance—both initially and along the way. Nonetheless the 40-20-40 can and generally does provide profound relief; but incorporating it into a shared life necessarily involves rough spots, stumbles, and sometimes even complete collapse. But the willingness to try again no matter how badly a particular attempt may blow up will yield new benefits every time.

What made Alexa and Dylan's relationship sane?

1. **Willingness** to put oneself into a reciprocal relationship with another person
2. **Development** and commitment to using those tools to cultivate a process of sharing equal responsibility for what happens in the relationship (the 40-20-40)
3. **Cultivating compassionate empathy**, which helps both parties learn to share loving and being loved in a relationship
4. **Allowing themselves** to feel loved and loveable in a measure that makes possible placing their hearts at risk for experiencing intimacy, empathy, and vulnerability

Exercise: Reframing Issues as Ours *(Couples)*

In the following exercise, return again to the issue you've been treating in the course of learning about the DREAM Sequence, paying particular attention to the Repair and Empowerment stages; only this time, refilter the issue through the lens of Mutuality. Scan for changes in how you perceive the issue once you see it as something you and your partner work on together as opposed to something you have to fix yourself.

Compare how you view the issue now with how you viewed it when you first started treating it with the exercises in this book. Use the following questions for your analysis, first individually and then sharing your responses as you've done in previous exercises.

- What differences do you now see in the part each of you plays?
- How do you now see each of your parts in the issue fitting together?
- What's different now in your overall perception of the issue?

Now comment on the following statements and questions.

- Unconditional openness to what each of us brings to the table improves our relationship and our ability to solve problems.
- What are my feelings about keeping my distance from my partner in the identified issue and in other parts of our relationship?
- How can what I've learned from doing the exercises change how our relationship functions overall?
- What specific attitudes and behaviors can I make part of my life to reverse and repair the harm I've caused my partner and our relationship? In other words, how can we build Mutuality into our everyday life together?

After you've shared your individual responses, pause to reflect on the idea of us-ness—what it means to see yourselves as *us* and how it changes sharing both day-to-day experiences and the inevitable rough spots that come with being together.

Use the following questions to explore how your understanding of the word *intimacy* has changed.

- How did your identified issue allow the two of you to avoid anxiety-provoking parts of your us-ness? How does buying into the idea of us-ness change that?
- How does the idea of us-ness change how you perceive the idea of taking care of your relationship? How do you feel about that?
- What attitudes and behaviors can you put into place jointly to cultivate us-ness—in other words, to nurture Mutuality?

Exercise: Mutuality *(Couples)*

The following exercise further develops a shared appreciation of Mutuality. Reflect upon and discuss the following questions.

- What is it like to see and feel yourselves choosing together to work through an issue that has had a long, significant impact on your shared life—or on your feelings about your shared life?
- How does it feel to commit to problem-solving *as a couple* as opposed to being left to cope with problems individually as best you can?

Before continuing, take this opportunity once again to use the Joint Compassion Meditation Exercise in Chapter 1.

- Set the timer for three to five minutes and relax in a seated position, bringing your attention to your breath while observing without judgment the stream of thoughts passing through your mind. Then return your attention to your breath.
- Remember that this is not about good/bad or right/wrong: it's *only* for becoming aware of what your mind does and cultivating the practice of stepping back from it.
- Now write down your thoughts, feelings, and insights. Be sure to include aspects about which you remain unsure or are not quite comfortable with: feeling that you can put those on the table safely is arguably the single most important aspect of practicing relationship sanity.
- Finally conduct a 40-20-40 based on your reflections on Mutuality as a problem-solving and relationship-grounding practice.

Staying on Target: Apart versus Together

Now, with a single focus that you're creating together, you can—one breath, one thought, and one task at a time—DREAM your way into a joint process of Mutuality that accompanies you every day in every part of your lives.

Key Takeaways

- We embrace the vitality of unpredictability and even the downsides of life as it "really is."
- We allow the giving and receiving, the helping and being helped, of reciprocal relationships.
- Self-Other Assessment is becoming part of our daily life—especially in our sharing and accountability
- We continue to grow as individuals and as collaborators in building relationship sanity.

Relationship sanity is, necessarily, dynamic and interactive. Understanding it so reveals it both as the labor and the fruit of the labor. Compulsive caretaking routines, on the other hand, protect couples from the things they both want and don't want. Irrelationship carefully keeps this tension, this ambivalence, below the radar so that you're protected from confronting your hope and dread.

Think of us-ness as mature adults who want and need care and affection while striving for synergy generated by healthy reliance, interdependency, and reciprocity—in short, Mutuality.

Now, once again, sit in a comfortable position, upright and relaxed. Look at each other long enough to get a sense of where your partner is or might be emotionally as you continue on the road of relationship sanity. The joint meditation process now focuses on Self-Other experience as means of creating Mutuality in which you exchange needed, desired, and effective care.

Next, using the free association tool, discuss any thoughts or thought fragments, feelings, and reflections on where you've been and where you're going on the road of relationship sanity.

Conclusion

The Road of Relationship Sanity

Perhaps the greatest irony of irrelationship versus relationship sanity is that, while irrelationship can feel safe even for periods of years, it leaves us disconnected, isolated, and lonely. Relationship sanity on the other hand, does the opposite: it puts us, individually and jointly, in direct connection with each other's feelings and needs. It's scary sometimes, but practicing mutual truth-telling quickly puts us in a space of safe, nurturing intimacy.

Exercise: How Has My Relationship with Irrelationship Changed? *(Couples)*

Following is a reprise of the self-assessment introduced in Chapter 2, which gives you an opportunity to revisit the same relationship markers drawn out in that exercise. Go through the questions first as individuals and then answer them together.

For each item, make notes about your feelings and replies, comparing how you view each item now with how you viewed the same item when you began working with this book.

After you've made your notes, share and discuss your responses with each other.

1. I should be the solution to my partner's life.
    a. Agree
    b. Not sure or sometimes
    c. Disagree

2. My partner should be the answer to what I need in my life.
    a. Agree
    b. Not sure or sometimes
    c. Disagree

3. Love mostly means taking care of my partner.
    a. Agree
    b. Not sure or sometimes
    c. Disagree

4. Love means my partner is always there to take care of me.
    a. Agree
    b. Not sure or sometimes
    c. Disagree

5. When I'm taking care of my partner, I sometimes feel unappreciated.
    a. Agree
    b. Not sure or sometimes
    c. Disagree

6. Things are too one-sided between my partner and me.
    a. Agree
    b. Not sure or sometimes
    c. Disagree

7. Being in a relationship is more work than pleasure.
   a. Agree
   b. Not sure or sometimes
   c. Disagree

8. My partner listens to me.
   a. Agree
   b. Not sure or sometimes
   c. Disagree

9. I usually feel that my relationship with my partner is a "plus" in my life.
   a. Agree
   b. Not sure or sometimes
   c. Disagree

Finally, extrapolating from the themes in items 1–9, discuss what has changed in your attitudes toward yourselves and each other since you've been working the DREAM Sequence.

Mai and Glen

Now back to Mai and Glen with an update on the art of healthy relationships.

"Well—it *does* seem to keep getting better," Mai said almost as if she wasn't sure it was safe to admit as much.

Glen agreed, "Yeah, but it makes me nervous to say so out loud! I'm afraid I'll jinx it!"

The word *intimacy* doesn't apply only to sexual relationships, although the bedroom is often the place where psychological defense is most apparent. As we've said, maintaining distance in that or any part of life requires cooperation by both parties. Happily, the converse is also true: one proof of the growth of relationship sanity is how it reinvigorates the simple act of touching, to say nothing of how it can reignite explicit eroticism.

Mai continued, "When we first started doing the work and telling each other things in the 40-20-40, it was a serious curveball. It was exhausting and even undercut our sex life for a while. It made me nervous because I was afraid you lost interest because you found out too much about me."

"Ha!" Glen replied. "I thought you were losing interest in *me*!"

Mai and Glen were feeling overwhelmed by both the care and the vulnerability they were experiencing at their partner's hands—feelings that often affect people who have been guarding themselves from one another for a prolonged period. It can become habitual to the point that they don't realize how much they miss the experience of deep partnership.

"But," Glen said, "even when it was like that, my heart still skipped a beat when I came home to you every day—like a buzz went through my whole body. But it scared me: I was so afraid of losing you, but I didn't know what to do, what to say. Remember when we first met? It was like that. I didn't know if I could survive being in love with you. But when I thought about losing you, I was *sure* I couldn't survive *that*. At the same time, I was afraid I might be 'going dead' the way it did with my first wife. Being with her got so boring, but that's never come close to happening with you. But I was still afraid I might have made some kind of mistake."

Just as distancing requires two, it takes two to make the solution—no matter what the issue is. As couples become experienced at practicing relationship sanity, they get ahead of it before it becomes a full-blown conflict—or a conflict at all. When they see it coming, the practiced couple (or even only one of them) calls time-out and asks for a spot-check inventory—an impromptu 40-20-40—to derail the fledgling conflict before it derails them. An added benefit is that couples who are able to trust one another in this process become increasingly comfortable with spontaneity and the unexpected in other parts of their lives—including the erotic.

This kind of skill building proved a major boon to Mai and Glen's life in the bedroom. The excitement of becoming increasingly truthful and vulnerable to one another added to their excitement—excitement that, even after twelve years of marriage, wasn't always easy for them to control in settings not suited for sexual intimacy. Conversely, the depth of their lovemaking pressed forward their eagerness to cultivate the habits that are the path of relationship sanity.

Many of us have lived our entire lives terrified that if we let someone we like get close, they'll find out too much about us and run the other way. Strangely though, risking letting someone else know about, or even see, our mistakes, missteps, and mess-ups is the key to getting cracked open to intimacy—another of irrelationship's choice ironies. But this isn't the case only because of the truth telling it involves: just as importantly, it gives us opportunity after opportunity to learn about one another's foibles and to accept each other's problematic decision-making, so we can find a way to use learning about things to create together a more honest, open life. In this way, love that had been a mixed fantasy complicated by our mistakes and fears turns into a shared journey beyond our wildest dreams.

A Final Word about the DREAM Sequence

The DREAM Sequence represents a synthesis of years of experience, both personal and professional, leading to the creation of tools that are both incisive and practical. When we first introduced it, we indicated that when going through the DREAM Sequence you would soon realize that calling it a sequence isn't quite accurate. The fact is that very little learning we undergo in our lives occurs strictly sequentially.

The DREAM Sequence is no different in that regard: it isn't a linear process with rules and tasks that must be completed correctly before you move on to the next stage. The reality is that once you have broken the ice with Discovery, each subsequent stage is likely to lead to discovery of more aspects of yourself and your relationships that have been distorted by irrelationship. As Empowerment moves forward, you will find more aspects of your shared life that need to be repaired. Creating Alternatives to your historic way of being together further increases individual and shared Empowerment. And the more comfortable you and your partner become with this process the more you will discover pieces of your individual and shared histories that you will want to disclose, explore, and repair. Thus the DREAM Sequence is a guide for the life-long, multidimensional process of being together in discovery, re-creation, and intimacy building that we call relationship sanity.

The Road of . . .

The Big Book of Alcoholics Anonymous (officially titled *Alcoholics Anonymous*) concludes with the line: ". . . and you will surely meet some of us as you trudge the Road of Happy Destiny".[1] Well known for being misquoted, the preposition *of* is often replaced with *to*, as if sobriety were a destination rather than a process and journey of growth. Similarly, relationship sanity is a process of repair and recovery from our detour into irrelationship.

The question "How do we get there?" has been answered: by joining with those from whom you've most carefully protected yourselves. Only now, you have the insight and tools for learning to allow them to be, to invite them to be, close in your lives in ways you've longed for and denied yourselves.

No longer insisting that the dynamics of your lives are manageable and certain, you can now allow yourselves lives that are stimulating, free, and unpredictable instead of carefully circumscribed by your fears of what might happen if you relinquish control.

Staying on Target: Irrelationship versus Relationship Sanity

Having completed your first pass at transforming your song-and-dance routine and your outlook on relationships, you are now recasting the word, "you" into the *us-ness* of relationship sanity.

Key Takeaways

- We've worked the DREAM Sequence together and are on the road of relationship sanity.
- We've learned about the practice of compassionate empathy by establishing our practice of the 40-20-40 and have seen for ourselves how it creates intimacy—sometimes from experiences with others that we had written off as irreparable.
- We've begun experiencing ourselves as a Self and as Self-Other and are taking responsibility for the well-being of that "third entity," our *us-ness*.
- Joint Compassionate Meditation is a method, one breath at a time, of DREAMing our way into a rich, sustained, everyday mutuality we had never imagined possible.
- The tools we've learned break through stifling isolation. When we feel ourselves returning to old patterns of isolation and fear, we now know how to use those tools and will stay together in the process of pulling ourselves back to each other.
- *Don't let the end of this book be the end of your journey:* write about and share your experience, telling others what it's been like to discover your own life as is!

Acknowledgments

As was the case with our first book, *Relationship Sanity* has many parents who have helped us and kept us on target in finding and staying on own way to, well, relationship sanity.

The foremost of those parents has also been the midwife: our agent, Gareth Esersky. Gareth consistently coaches—and sometimes referees—us toward a richer vision of our own work that we wouldn't likely be able to achieve if left to our own designs.

The team at Central Recovery Press (CRP), especially Valerie Killeen, Nancy Schenck, Patrick Hughes, and Janet Ottenweller, have been indispensible as mentors in different aspects of this singular project. Their hearts and skills have proven a gratifying fit. The shared values, particularly a commitment to health and helping individuals recover from addiction and trauma, has created the best possible fit between CRP and this team of researchers/clinicians/authors.

We would also like to thank Tamara Connolly of We Are How for her fantastic design work—and that rockin' logo!

From Mark Borg

Along with the acknowledgments mentioned above, I want to thank and thank and thank my family: my wife and soul mate, love of my life, Haruna, and our beloved grrrrrrls, Kata and Uta. All three have given me, most primarily and consistently, the love that is and has been the inspiration for my part of this continuing project. Giving and receiving love, loving and being loved, begins at home with these three, and this relationship sanity is with me in every step of this walk that we take through our everyday lives—together.

Similarly, the care that I am honored to provide for my patients in my practice challenges me each day to provide care and simultaneously accept the care that my patients give to me through their ongoing trust and willingness to work through all that is—and has been—what brought them into psychoanalytic treatment.

This is a book about love, in many ways it is a kind of love letter—expressing a reciprocity that is isomorphic to what's going on in these pages—to all of those who have loved and been loved by me.

Over the years, the categories—work and love—have blurred. There has been so much love given and received between, within, and among the variety of contexts, communities, and settings that I've experienced that I am now overwhelmed by the task of allowing myself to feel all this support, care, and love as I am allowing myself to re-experience the ways in which I have been—and am still—*held* by these relationships.

I need to begin by thanking my maternal grandmother, Charlotte Rolland, whose love carried me through the most difficult of times and who, I continue to believe, implanted a love in my heart that continues to allow me to survive and thrive through good times and bad. My father's father, Ed Borg, also loved my mother, my brother, and me—no matter what—through the tumult of my early life, and I remain grateful.

Thank you to my mom and stepfather to whom this book is dedicated, as well as to my father, Mark Borg, and his amazingly warm, kind, and generous wife, Bonnie Mankoff. Thank you, Uncle Erik and Aunt Sandy, for caring for and listening to me. I thank you Aunt Sandy, in particular, for courageously confronting a wild teenager at some particularly tricky crossroads and showing me a glimpse of a reality I'd not have been able to consider, much less see. As always, sending much love to my brother, Chris—among the kindest, most generous, souls I've known.

Then there was the anarchy in the OC: the surfers, the mods, the punks, the artists, the dreamers—the winter sea and a gang of grommets paddling out into thwalpin' breakers. Living like *Lord of the Flies* across and within all those harrowing scenes. How did we survive? Love and gratitude—again and again—to our band, All Nite Rave, my earliest inspiration for putting pen to paper. And when gratitude goes out to that band and all that teenage angst—"I want you, I do, almost as much as I don't"—my biggest love goes out to you, Jim DeLozier, and your parents, Joan and Terry, who took me in when all seemed lost.

Much gratitude to a host of wandering/wondering souls who shoulder-to-shouldered my early days of writing and developing some kind of verve for this kind of thing: Britt Huycke, William Defina, Scott Murdock, Megan Hardy, Karin Nance, Darren Ribant, Elizabeth Shanahan, Alex Siu, Mike Ferguson, Carrie Burnett, Matt Dalton, Jim Stauffer, Scott Parker, David Jawor, Rob Hillis, Scott Stewart, Dave Collins, and Tim Barnes.

And, there through it all, my very first muse and soul mate (as each of those listed here is): Kristy Matthews—Q of S, K in O (now H). The currency of love that you've consistently sent to me through almost all my life continues to inspire and sustain me.

Thank you, Daniel MacNamee, no way I'm getting through boot camp and airborne school (Fort Benning) or air assault training (Fort Campbell) without you. And thank you, John Henry Eldridge, Brendan Rafferty, Tim Couch, David Lester, Karen Puckett, and Sean Carver for helping me survive everything else as we were *rolling down the chamber*.

A chance 6:00 a.m. encounter in San Francisco, 1991, resulted in me running into another soul mate, Mike Dalla, with whom I've been in an almost every day conversation—filled with love, camaraderie, and belly-laughing bliss—ever since. I love watching you raise your beautiful girls and am eternally grateful that we have been able to trudge our way through this life together for all these days, months, years, and now decades.

John (Purple) Turi gets special mention as he was with whom I charged that SoCal surf many years ago—wearing the dog shoes as we carved the "no matter what" backdoor barrel! You are a writer/artist/poet whose mind and heart twists and turns in ways that have intrigued and inspired me for decades, as well as another long-lost brother with whom I fear I could not live without.

Bill Zunkel, what can I say? Love at first sight? Indeed. We have traveled the world and loved each other every day since that "chance encounter" at that coffee urn in Sunset Beach. Thank you for joining me in so many, many harrowing adventures.

Of course, there is my coauthor, Danny Berry—a soul mate whose steady hand and willingness to join me in what, every day, seems and feels like a brand-new world, a world of loving and being loved, giving and receiving—serves as a primary inspiration for whatever it is that allows us, allows me, to work my way through being stuck in my own song-and-dance routine.

Happy to have met you, Matt Stedman, because I know of no one else who is willing to brave those freezing Atlantic seas as we surf through the East Coast winters together!

Thanks to 12th Street, Chapter Nine, and the Seal Beach Surf Crew—especially my enduring pals, Greg Hex, Jason Kaja, and Scott Munsey.

A few other trudgers who gave—and give—light to my journey: Chris Mertz, Isa Stanfiels, Phil Vock, Paul Loranger, Byron Abel, Molly Goldman, Paul Tulley, Jose (Cheo) Rodriguez, Liz Rusch, Vic Ruggiero, Johanna Rhyins, Wil Diaz, Shawn Marie Turi, Eric Lee, Marty Strom, Ken Robidoux, Emily Garrod, Mik Manenti, Stuart Pyle, Thomas Cox, Emily Damron, Paco and Maiken Lozano-Wiese, Daniel Leyva, John Hatchett, Chana Pollack, Rob Gutfleisch, Helmut Krackie, Scott Graham, James Petty, James Kwon, James Gary, Sr., Pat Kenary, Bobbi Fuentes, Mary Jane Rambo, Richie Velez, Michael Lynch, Gene Magnetti, Elise Cox, David Kopstein, John Ellert, Mark Lanaghan, Ronnie Sawyer, Adrian Sutton, Glen Parish, Steve Torrey, Kim and Wendy Marshall, and Kelley Marshall-Smoot.

I am brimming over with gratitude for the professional mentors/colleagues/muses who have supported and cared for me throughout the last—my first—thirty years of working in the mental health field. Joseph

Solomita for giving me my first chance at Newport Harbor Adolescent Psychiatric Hospital; Jeanne Henry for taking me under her wing there, mentoring me and remaining a dear friend; Dr. Maggie Decker for hiring me at AIDS Service Foundation, an experience that opened me up to experiences of love and empathy I'd previously not known could be possible. Thank you, Dr. Roger Mills, for giving me the chance to work with you in the Community Health Realization Institute, which implemented a four-year post-crisis, empowerment program in Avalon Garden, South Central, Los Angeles, after the riots in 1992. Which brings me to my professional soul mate, Dr. Ronda Hampton, with whom I worked shoulder-to-shoulder throughout the entirety of the South Central project. Thank you, Dr. Stanley Graham, for inviting me to work at The Fifth Avenue Center in the West Village of New York City—which turned out to be the move that landed me, professionally and personally, in the city that did, and does, move with the beating of my heart. Thank you Joerg Bose, my training analyst at William Alanson White Institute for Psychiatry, Psychology, and Psychoanalysis. Thank you to my training supervisors: Brian Sweeney, Carola Mann, Jack Drescher, Sandra Buechler, and Sue Kolod. And, finally, thank you Eve Golden for holding my hand and walking with me through every step of my entre into the realm of writing academically and professionally—I love you.

Finally, thanks again to Grant Brenner and Danny Berry (DB-san, in a double acknowledgment). Though we don't always agree, I've said many times that the closest parallel I've found to this project—and my sense of relating to the two of you throughout this project—is marriage. Like marriage, we've spanned the continuum from irrelationship to relationship sanity innumerable times. And like marriage—or any other relationship that threatens intimacy—our team has provided immense opportunities to work through irrelationship dynamics. And so, I am grateful that our partnership has survived, and sometimes thrived, to allow us to continue to trudge this road of relationship sanity together.

From Daniel Berry

I also want to thank my coworkers, especially Danny, Stephen, and Ace, who have always had my back as I found my way through the process of making a book.

I'm also grateful for friends, associates, and others who provided feedback that consistently validated the work that Mark, Grant, and I set out to do.

And of course, I want to thank James for the understated but loving way that he supports and encourages me, no matter what I do—or don't do.

Notes

Introduction

1. Everyone faces life crises that test our resilience and resolve as individuals and couples. Those occasions increase the risk for activating irrelationship dynamics. In fact, Terror Management Theory (TMT) and the related idea of mortality salience provide a vocabulary for reflecting on how and why we sometimes use maladaptive defenses to cope in crisis rather than deliberately setting out to make better choices. According to TMT, serious threats will even cause individuals to shift their worldview in order to maintain self-esteem during a crisis. Such life events include

   - illness of oneself or loved ones;

   - financial problems;

   - issues related to having children, such as whether to have or how many; infertility; loss of a child or fetus; and illness in a child and others;

   - infidelity;

   - sexual dissatisfaction;

   - career changes, such as forced to consider relocating for one partner's job loss, failure to realize professional goals, and other job-related disturbances.

2. The concept of "third entity" is inspired by Thomas Ogden's concept of the *analytic third* (Ogden, 1994, pp. 3–4). This refers to a third subject, unconsciously co-created by therapist and client, which seems to take on a life of its own in the interpersonal field between them. This third subject stands in dialectical tension with the separate, individual subjectivities of analyst and analysand in such a way that the individual subjectivities and the third create, negate, and preserve one another. In an analytic relationship, the notion of individual subjectivity and the idea of a co-created third subject are devoid of meaning except in relation to one another, just as the idea of the conscious mind is meaningless except in relation to the unconscious.

3. Freud, "Group Psychology and the Analysis of the Ego," 69.

Although renowned for his pessimistic view of human psychology, with humans being at odds with each other and ourselves, at one point Freud himself acknowledged the thoroughly relational and interdependent nature of human existence: "The contrast between individual psychology and social or group psychology, which at first glance may seem full of significance, loses a great deal of its sharpness when it is examined more closely. It is true that individual psychology is concerned with the individual man and explores the paths by which he seeks to find satisfaction for his instinctual impulses; but only rarely and under certain exceptional conditions is individual psychology in a position to disregard the relations of this individual to others. In the individual's mental life someone else is invariably involved, as a model, as an object, as a helper, as an opponent; and so from the very first, individual psychology, in this extended but entirely justified sense of the word, is at the same time social psychology as well."

4. Fromm, *The Art of Loving*, 18–19.

5. The development of the concept of brainlock relies, most especially, on neuroscientific research conducted by Gaetan de Lavilléon, Marie Masako Lacroix, Laure Rondi-Reig, and Karim Benchenane, 2015, pp. 493–495; Klimecki, O. M., Leilberg, S., Lamm, C. & Singer, T., 2013, pp. 1552–61; and Allan Schore, 2008, pp. 9–20.

6. Sullivan, *The Interpersonal Theory of Psychiatry*, 22.

Harry Stack Sullivan, the founder of interpersonal psychoanalytic theory, observed that human beings have an in-born motivational system to be a care-seeker and heal the wounds of those who provide us with comfort and security. As wounds are relational, so must the healing process be. Sullivan wrote, in what is referred to as the *One-Genus Postulate*, "Everyone is much more simply human than otherwise." Sullivan believed that there is no human experience that is beyond comprehension, and with enough understanding—specifically to the social circumstances underlying our problems—just about anyone could be helped. Sullivan was, in many ways, suggesting that we co-create mental illness and mental health.

7. Carnes, Laaser, and Laaser, *Open Hearts*, 98.

8. Freud, "Remembering, Repeating and Working Though," 150.

Freud states that "the patient remembers nothing of what is forgotten or repressed, but . . . he expresses it in action. He reproduces it not in his memory but in his behavior; he repeats it, but without of course knowing that he is repeating it."

9. Searles, "The Patient as Therapist to His Analyst." 95

10. Bowlby, "The Nature of the Child's Tie to His Mother." 354.

11. Johnson, *Love Sense*, 38.

12. The 40-20-40 Model has been developed to be used as a kind of *couple's inventory*, but it was adapted from work done earlier by Dr. Borg in a community revitalization/empowerment program from what we called *Group Process Empowerment* (Borg, 2001, 2010). We found that it is an extremely effective means for helping people during difficult times in their relationship, to hit pause, establish a peaceful, safe place, and account together for where it was that things went *off the rails*. The 40-20-40 is an opportunity to *get it back on the rails together*. It is a way to re-establish peace in a relationship. In this work—though couples won't necessarily have the active and overt participation of "the world"—they still believe they can use the 40-20-40 to establish safe places for themselves to come to terms with what in the world, in their lives, they can and cannot do something about (Borg, 2002, 2003, 2004, 2010).

Chapter 1

1. Žižek, *Žižek's Jokes*, 47.

2. The joint compassionate empathy and intimacy exercises throughout this book are inspired by and adapted from Mindful Self-Compassion Program (MSC) by Chris Germer and Kristen Neff (in Singer and Bolz, *Compassion: Bridging Practice and Science*, 365–396).

3. Germer and Neff, "The Mindful Self-Compassion Training Program (MSC)," 367.

Chapter 2

1. Mitchell, *Can Love Last?*, 91–92.

2. Ainsworth, "The Development of Infant-Mother Attachment," 11–13; Bowlby, *Attachment and Loss*, 353.

3. Bowlby, "The Nature of the Child's Tie to His Mother," 362.

4. Bowlby, "The Nature of the Child's Tie to His Mother," 362.

Chapter 3

1. This exercise is inspired and adapted from Chris Germer and Kristen Neff.

Chapter 4

1. Fairbairn, *An Object-Relations Theory of Personality*, 145.

The object-relations psychoanalyst Ronald Fairbairn designates the full development of emotional health as the stage of mature dependence. Healthy adults are emotionally interdependent upon each other.

Chapter 5

1. Žižek, *Žižek's Jokes*, p. 47.

Chapter 8

1. What is an acting-out behavior? Actually, it is just about anything we do that somehow communicates something we are feeling without our awareness of what we are feeling. Truth be told, our minds know that we do not need to actually feel absolutely everything we *feel*. There is much that is going on within us emotionally that is allowed to bypass our actual awareness—even our experience—of it.

2. Resentment seems to be the feeling that bridges the gap, the feeling that is most consistent in both the Performer and the Audience. It is the feeling that most effectively covers up the isolation, and the feeling that simultaneously makes the isolation so easy to acknowledge, to deal with, to treat.

3. Sunk cost fallacy: Because sunk costs are already spent and cannot be recovered, it is irrational to consider the value of sunk costs when considering alternative actions. Future actions cannot reverse past losses. Economics and business decision-making recognize *sunk costs* as the costs that have already been incurred and which can never be recovered to any significant degree. Economic theory proposes that a rational actor does not let sunk costs influence a decision because past costs cannot be recovered in any case. This is also called the *bygones principle*; let bygones be bygones. This recognizes that you cannot change the past. The *fallacy of sunk costs* is to consider sunk costs when making a decision. Sound business decisions are based on a forward-looking view, ignoring sunk costs. Unfortunately human beings continue to value a past investment of money, effort or some intangible quality (e.g., "credibility" or "face") independent of the investment's probability of paying future dividends. The irrelevance of sunk costs is a well-known principle of business and economics, but common behavior often ignores this fallacy of trying to undo the past. For example, revenge is an attempt to recover the sunk costs that represent some past and irrevocable harm or loss. People falsely reason, "I have too much invested to quit now" when it is rational to only look at the future prospects of the activity. Arguing, "we must continue to fight to honor those who have already died" is another tragic but appealing fallacy of sunk costs.

4. We act-out in all kinds of ways, all the time. The term *acting out* gets a pretty bad rap in our society, but really, by the time we are telling our husband or

wife or kid that he or she is acting out (i.e., drinking too much, taking drugs, checking out an abundance of internet porn), we usually mean that he or she is either doing something (1) destructive (to self and/or other) or (2) we think is wrong. That's usually all there is to it; therefore, in its general use, the term does not only cover the vast array of ways in which acting out can be utilized to express things that are too bothersome, painful, terrifying (or, most importantly, that we think make us look like "bad people" in the eyes of others) to contemplate or are simply too insignificant to be registered consciously.

Chapter 10

1. When we wrote to "Olivia" to ask for her permission to include her story, she wrote back with her consent and said, "I'm 50 now, sober 19 years, and in that 'A' love that you told me about—the 10 out of 10."

Chapter 11

1. The social psychologist and social psychologist, Erich Fromm believed that "All are in need of help and depend on one another. Human solidarity is the necessary condition for the unfolding of any one individual" (*Escape From Freedom*, p. 101). This is a guiding principle for understanding interactive repair and a reminder of why we must continue to grapple with the pain and uncertainty of working through irrelationship—to find each other and to find ourselves.

2. Tronick, "Emotions and Emotional Communication in Infants," 112–119.

Chapter 12

1. Rappaport and Seidman, *Handbook of Community Psychology*, xiii.

2. Winnicott, *Collected Papers*, 186.

3. Borg, "The Avalon Gardens Men's Association," 347.

4. Borg, "Heist-ing the Analyst's Penis (at Gunpoint)," 77.

   "Character is the sum in each of us of the need to seek security and the need to avoid anxiety."

Chapter 13

1. Gottman, *The Marriage Clinic*, 68.

2. Gottman and Gottman, *10 Principles for Doing Effective Couples Therapy*, 18–19.

3. The earliest writings about the "Dirty Dozen" were in Thomas Gordon's book, *T.E.T: Teacher Effectiveness Training* (1977). He called them "Communication Roadblocks." Many authors have picked up on Gordon's list, as we have, elaborating and clarifying them, and adapting them to specific situations (e.g., management, relationships, etc.).

Chapter 14

1. Carnes, Laaser, and Laaser, *Open Hearts*, 98.

Conclusion

1. Alcoholics Anonymous, *Alcoholics Anonymous*, 164.

Bibliography

Ainsworth, Mary. "The Development of Infant-Mother Attachment." In *Review of Child Development Research, Child Development and Social Policy Volume 3*, edited by Bettye Cardwell and Henry N. Ricciuti, 1–94. Chicago: University of Chicago Press, 1973.

Alcoholics Anonymous. *Alcoholics Anonymous*. New York: Alcoholics Anonymous World Services. Inc., 2001.

Borg, Jr., Mark B. "The Avalon Gardens Men's Association: A Community Health Psychology Case Study." *Journal of Health Psychology* 7, no. 3 (2002): 345–57.

Borg, Jr., Mark B. "Community Group-Analysis: A Post-Crisis Synthesis." *Group-Analysis* 36, no. 2 (2003): 228–41.

Borg, Jr., Mark B. "Venturing Beyond the Consulting Room: Psychoanalysis in Community Crisis Intervention." *Contemporary Psychoanalysis* 40, no. 2 (2004): 147–74.

Borg, Jr., Mark B. "Community Psychoanalysis: Developing a Model of Psychoanalytically-Informed Community Crisis Intervention." In *Community Psychology: New Directions*, edited by Niklas Lange and Marie Wagner, 1–66. Hauppauge, NY: Nova Science Publishers, 2010.

Borg, Jr., Mark B. "Heist-ing the Analyst's Penis (at Gunpoint): Community Enactment in the Treatment of an FtM Trasngendered Analysand." *International Journal of Transgenderism*, 13 no. 2 (2011): 77-90.

Borg, Jr., Mark B., Grant H. Brenner, and Daniel Berry. *Irrelationship: How We Use Dysfunctional Relationships to Hide from Intimacy*. Las Vegas, NV: Central Recovery Press, 2015.

Bowlby, John. "The Nature of the Child's Tie to His Mother." *International Journal of Psychoanalysis*, 39 (1958): 350–71.

Bowlby John. *Attachment and Loss Volume 1: Attachment.* New York: Basic Books, 1969.

Carnes, Patrick, Debra Laaser, and Mark Laaser. *Open Hearts: Renewing Relationships with Recovery, Romance and Reality.* Wickenburg, AZ: Gentle Path Press, 1999.

de Lavilléon, Gaetan, Marie Masako Lacroix, Laure Rondi-Reig, and Karim Benchenane. "Explicit Memory Creation During Sleep Demonstrates a Causal Role of Place Cells in Navigation." *Nature Neuroscience* 18 (March 2015): 493–495. doi: 10.1038/nn.3970.

Fairbairn, W. Ronald D. *An Object-Relations Theory of Personality.* New York: Basic Books, 1952.

Freud, Sigmund. "Remembering, Repeating and Working Though." In *Standard Edition of the Complete Works of Sigmund Freud, Vol. 12*, 145–56. London: The Hogarth Press, 1914.

Freud, Sigmund. "Group Psychology and the Analysis of the Ego." In *Standard Edition of the Complete Works of Sigmund Freud, Vol. 18*, 67–144. London: The Hogarth Press, 1921.

Fromm, Erich. *Escape From Freedom.* New York: Holt, Rinehart & Winston, 1941.

Fromm, Erich. *The Art of Loving.* New York: Harper & Row, 1956.

Germer, Chris and Kristen Neff. "The Mindful Self-Compassion Training Program (MSC)"; In Tania Singer and Matthias Bolz (2013) (eds.) *Compassion: Bridging Practice and Science* (pp. 365–396). Munich, Germany: Max-Planck Society.

Gordon, Thomas. *T.E.T: Teacher Effectiveness Training.* Toronto, Ontario, Canada: Addison-Wesley-Longman Ltd, 1977.

Gottman, John M. *The Marriage Clinic.* New York: W.W. Norton, 1999.

Gottman, Julie S. and John M. Gottman. *10 Principles for Doing Effective Couples Therapy.* New York: W.W. Norton, 2015.

Johnson, Sue. *Love Sense: The Revolutionary New Science of Romantic Relationships.* New York: Little, Brown and Company, 2013.

Klimecki, O. M., Leilberg, S., Lamm, C. & Singer, T. (2013). Functional neural plasticity and associated changes in positive affect after compassion training. *Cerebral Cortex, 23*, 1552-61.

Mitchell, Stephen. A. *Can Love Last?: The Fate of Romance over Time.* New York: W.W. Norton, 2002.

Ogden, Thomas. "The Analytic Third: Working with Intersubjective Clinical Facts." *International Journal of Psycho-Analysis* 75 (1994): 3–20.

Rappaport, Julian and Edward Seidman, eds. *Handbook of Community Psychology*. New York: Kluwer Academic/Plenum Publishers, 2000.

Schore, Judtih R. and Allan N. Schore. (2008). Modern attachment theory: the central role of affect regulation in development and treatment. *Clinical Social Work Journal, 36,* 9-20.

Searles, Harold. "The Patient as Therapist to His Analyst." In *Tactics and Techniques in Psychoanalytic Therapy: Volume II Countertransference*, edited by Peter L. Giovacchini, 95-151. New York: Aronson, 1975.

Singer, Tania and Matthias Bolz, eds. *Compassion: Bridging Practice and Science*. Munich: Max Planck Society, 2013.

Sullivan, Harry Stack. *The Interpersonal Theory of Psychiatry*. New York: W.W. Norton, 1953.

Tronick, Edward Z. "Emotions and Emotional Communication in Infants." *American Psychologist* 44, no. 2 (1989): 112–19.

Winnicott, Donald W. *Collected Papers: Through Paediatrics to Psycho-Analysis*. London: Tavistock Publications, 1958.

Winnicott, Donald W. *The Maturational Process and the Facilitating Environment*. New York: International Universities Press, 1965.

Žižek, Slavoj. *Žižek's Jokes: Did You Hear the One About Hegel and Negation?* Cambridge, MA: The MIT Press, 2014.

About the Authors

Mark B. Borg, Jr., PhD, has practiced in New York City as a licensed psychologist and psychoanalyst since 1998. He relocated to New York from Los Angeles after working for three years in South Central Los Angeles following the 1992 riots, developing theories and implementation strategies for community crisis intervention. This project received Congressional commendation and led to Dr. Borg's cofounding the Community Consulting Group, a firm that trains community stakeholders and other players in the use of psychoanalytical techniques for community rebuilding and revitalization. Dr. Borg's writings on community intervention, organizational consultation, and application of psychoanalytic theory to community crisis intervention have been published in various journals and collected work, and he has presented papers on his theories at academic conferences in the United States, Canada, Scotland, Ireland, Norway, Italy, Greece, Turkey, South Africa, Chile, and Israel.

Grant Hilary Brenner, MD, is a psychiatrist, psychoanalyst, and consultant in New York City. In private practice since 2002, he focuses on the treatment of adults facing serious difficulties in relationships, professional endeavors, and personal development, integrating multiple approaches to provide personalized care. Dr. Brenner takes a pragmatic and realistically optimistic position: People have the capacity to thrive and also have untapped strength and resilience. He teaches and supervises residents and therapists, is editor of the book *Creating Spiritual and Psychological Resilience—Integrating Care in Disaster Relief Work*, and is involved in not-for-profit work with Disaster Psychiatry Outreach as Vice President of the Board of Directors and as Co-Chair of the Disasters and the World Committee: Group for the Advancement of Psychiatry. He is an Assistant Clinical Professor of Psychiatry at Mount Sinai Beth Israel and Director of the Trauma Service at the William Alanson White Institute, in addition to other roles. For additional information, please visit GrantHBrennerMD.com

Daniel Berry, RN, MHA, has practiced as a Registered Nurse in New York City since 1987. Working in inpatient, home care, and community settings, his work has taken him into some of the most privileged households as well as some of its most marginalized public housing projects in Manhattan and the South Bronx. He is currently Assistant Director of Nursing for Risk Management at a public facility serving homeless and undocumented victims of street violence, addiction, and traumatic injuries. In 2015, he was invited to serve as a nurse consultant to a United Nations-certified NGO in Afghanistan promoting community development and addressing women's and children's health issues.